America the the Racist?

Volume One

New Paradigm Publishing
P.O. Box 302
Wilmington, North Carolina 28402

Third Printing: September 2008
Second Printing: April 2008
First Printing: September 2006

Published by:
New Paradigm Publishing   SAN: 255-8440
P.O. Box 302
Wilmington, NC 28402
(800) 570-4009

Email: connections477@earthlink.net

Copyright © 2006, 2008 by H. J. Harris

Library of Congress Cataloging-in-Publication Data

Harris, H. J., 1944-
    America The Racist, Volume One / by
H. J. Harris
      p.   cm.
      ISBN   0-9748362-5-7   paperback edition
      ISBN 978-0-9748362-5-6

1. United States —Race relations.
2. United States—Social conditions
3. United States—Politics and government
4. African American—Social conditions
5. Racism—United States

Prologue

As we experienced the political battle between Barak Obama and Hillary Clinton and anticipate the battle between Obama and John McCain, the issue of race in America continually takes center stage. Sometime the race issue is front and center as with the comments of Rev. Jeremiah Wright, Obama's minister for many years.

Generally, the response of white Americans was anger, disgust, and vicious attacks on Rev. Wright. White Americans rarely dealt with the historical context on which Rev. Wright's comments were made. They were incensed that a Black American minister would speak disparagingly about America and its treatment of black Americans.

Black Americans, on the other hand, could identify with much of what Rev. Wright had said because many of them had felt the pain of injustice, discrimination, and racism.

White Americans could not understand the rage that Rev. Wright expressed in his sermon because, to paraphrase the words of Frederick Douglas, they have never spent one day as a slave, as a second-class citizen, as the victim of vicious, ungodly racism.

At other times the racism is more subtle, more sublime – like the *"Bradley Factor"*. When Tom Bradley ran for Governor of California in 1982, the polls were showing a comfortable lead for certain victory. When the votes were counted, Bradley lost.

The Bradley Factor describes a phenomenon wherein white voters say one thing to political pollsters about voting for a black American – professing a non-racist attitude. When these same white voters get into the secrecy of the voting booth, they vote the opposite – expressing a subtle, hidden racism that exists in the American reality.

Many black Americans see the Clinton – Obama battle, and presumably the McCain - Obama contest as a crucial test of the conscience and moral fiber of America.

Obama sees victory based on America - the United States of America - living up to its creed and promise that *"all men are created equal. . ."*. In the imagery of Dr. Martin Luther King, Jr. in his *I Have A Dream* speech, Obama is presenting the great check to America and expecting it to clear - *paid in full*.

Many black Americans believe that Hillary Clinton's dogged determination to stay in the race for president, although numerically she could not win in the delegate count, was based on a belief in the *"Bradley Factor"*.

There is a strong belief in the black American community that Clinton's statements that she is most electable - that she is the one who can win in the November 2008 presidential election - is a coded, euphemistic way of saying that in the final analysis, white Americans will not vote for a black American man to lead this country.

Regardless of the polls and the voter excitement about Obama's candidacy, this presidential election will be a true test of the moral fiber of America.

Will white and black Americans be able to step into the voting booth and choose a black American man over a white American man to lead this country?

Will we as Americans be able to overcome the cancer of racism that has afflicted this country for over

200 years?

Can we judge the presidential candidates by the content of their character rather than the color of their skin?

Black Americans fear that some white Americans, in the privacy of the voting booth - when their actions are between them and their God alone - will once again succumb to racist prejudice and vote for anyone but the black American man.

The purpose of this book is to put forth a brief, historical, spiritual, and psychological treatment of Racism in America - its causes, evolution, and possibilities for the future. Once we understand why we are where we are as a nation, then we are better equipped to determine what we must do to become the *"one Nation under God"* described in Dr. King's dream and in the Pledge of Allegiance.

The outcome of the Obama – McCain presidential campaign will be a final test of the moral conscience of America and our true commitment to the words and spirit set forth in the Declaration of Independence – ***"that all men are created equal ... with certain inalienable rights ... Life, Liberty, and the pursuit of Happiness"***.

Table of Contents

Dedication

This book is dedicated to all who have suffered the brutality of slavery, the injustice of discrimination, and the pain of dreams deferred.

Introduction

The purpose of this book is to demonstrate and explain to citizens of the world that racism is at the root and core of every aspect of American life. As long as racism exists in the psyche of this country, America's claims of moral authority will be hollow and disingenuous.

America the Racist, the title of this book, is a parody of the poem and song, *"America the Beautiful"* by Katharine Lee Bates, Melody by Samuel Ward
The first verse of the poem states:

> *O Beautiful for spacious skies*
> *For amber waves of grain*
> *For purple mountain majesties*
> *Above the fruited plain!*
> *America! America!*
> *God shed his grace on thee*
> *And crown thy good with brotherhood*
> *From sea to shining sea!"*

It is ironic that the great singer Ray Charles, a black American, did a soulful version of *"America the Beautiful"* that sold many records and CD's and brought tears to the eyes of many listeners.

The events surrounding the treatment of black Americans in New Orleans, Louisiana as a result of hurricane Katrina rekindled feelings of injustice and inequality experienced by many black Americans. This tragic event reminded the entire world that America – those in power who control the country – to this very day, treat black Americans as they always have – as second-class citizens.

The slow response to the plight of black Americans stranded without food, water, or humane accommodations for over four days—as the world looked on in shock, horror, and disbelief—reminded us that, for many of those in power in America, *"crowning thy good with brotherhood"* so loftily proclaimed in *"America the Beautiful"* **applies only to white Americans.**

TV footage of black Americans stranded for days on roof tops without food or water in the heart of the richest nation on earth reminded the world of the true attitude and feelings toward the needs of black Americans by those in power in America.

A new generation of world citizens—people who live outside of America—watched the Katrina Affair in shock, horror, disbelief and puzzlement. They must have asked themselves: "How could America, the country that holds itself out as a bastion of justice and freedom, let this happen to her citizens—her black citizens?"

Why was America paralyzed for over four days from bringing aid to black Americans, while it could easily get aid and medical supplies to foreigners halfway around the globe within 48 to 72 hours?

The answer is the same now, in the twenty-first century, as it was in the 1960's when billy-clubs of racist white police officers cracked the skulls and bones of black Americans; when groups of white police officers had trained-dogs viciously tear the flesh from the bodies of innocent black Americans who were trying to integrate the public schools and obtain the life, liberty, justice, and pursuit of happiness promised in the United States Constitution.

From the depths of their being, the powers that control America are quite content to treat black Americans as though they were a sub-human species with no rights that a white man is obligated to respect.

Whether in the 1960's or today, the primary reason that white American people in power respond to the needs, circumstances and conditions of black Americans, is to maintain a façade to the world that America is truly *"one nation under God with liberty and justice for all."*

Let us look at the Pledge of Allegiance recited throughout America by school children and government officials before the conduct of official business.

The Pledge of Allegiance

*I pledge allegiance to the Flag
of the United States of America,
and to the Republic for which it stands:
one Nation under God, indivisible,
With Liberty and Justice for all.*

When Americans recite *The Pledge of Allegiance*, there is a sense of a great contradiction: many white Americans know that Liberty and Justice for all is illusion, and most black Americans know that Liberty and Justice for all is a lie.

The way America has and still does treat black Americans is the great contradiction that undermines its credibility and moral authority in the global world.

The Truth about America

If the world only knew the truth about America:

America is a country built on the tortured bodies of black men who were stolen in the night from their homeland Africa.

America is a country where black women were systematically raped, abused and disrespected in ways no God fearing person could even imagine.

America is a country where, between 1882 and 1968, there were 3446 recorded lynchings of black American men and women. These statistics translate into 40 black Americans lynched per year, or one (1) black American lynched every 9 days over a total of 86 years.

This *"official"* number of lynchings is very conservative since many lynchings of black Americans were never reported. Lynchings were often led by the upstanding, prominent Christian white men who had black men and women hung from trees, their bodies burned, mutilated and dismembered—often on hot Sunday afternoons, after church and prayer—with little white boys and girls observing these lynching.

In this way these curious boys and girls could learn, know, and understand how black people could be treated at a white man's whim and fancy.

Lynching in America was a ritual of interracial social control and sadistic sport rather than simply a punishment for a crime.

America is a country where some white people have done everything possible to keep black Americans in perpetual subjugation, or destroy them if they resist, while other white people stand by watching in quiet acquiescence.

America is a country that must put its own

house in order before going out to the world preaching truth, justice, democracy, and fair play.

Black Americans Survive

Black Americans, whose ancestors were kidnapped Africans, continue to survive as vivid reminders of the true soul of America that reveals itself to the world in situations like Hurricane Katrina.

And yet, in spite of all that America has done to black Americans, these *kidnapped Africans* have survived to testify and tell their story about the truth of America.

The Kidnapped African Would Not Die!
By H. J. Harris

As the period of the great captivity draws to a close, there is a deep yearning to re-establish that ancestral connection between Africans of the Homeland, who were spared the middle passage, and the kidnapped Africans who now populate the shores of America.

The Kidnapped Africans began their involuntary journey into the great captivity afflicted with the endless horror of being taken in the night from their families and loved ones. They were dragged across the body of Mother Africa in chains, in pain, in fear of a terrible bondage from which there was no escape but death.

Mighty warriors were hunted and trapped by godless cowards without valor, respect, or conscience. Descendants of kings and prophets were captured in nets, placed in chains, then subjected to the operation of a coward's vanity and ego.

Oh! it must have been some feeling of vile ex-

hilaration for the vicious slave hunter to watch proud African men of royal descent broken down, beaten, and tortured to the rhythm of constant pain systematically inflicted.

BUT, THE KIDNAPPED AFRICAN WOULD NOT DIE!

Beautiful African women were kidnapped from the bosom of Mother Africa - torn from her magnificent breasts and taken across an ocean of tears to a hostile land which gave her no respect or praise.

In the new world, the Kidnapped African was whipped, tortured, and mutilated into submission or death. Those who survived this cruel destruction of body, mind and spirit became the slaves of America. This dehumanizing process transformed the Kidnapped African into human property to be possessed and used at the whims and fancies of a heartless master.

BUT, THE KIDNAPPED AFRICAN WOULD NOT DIE!

The transformation of the Kidnapped African into the American slave had as its intent the total destruction of the African mind, consciousness, and spirit. Penetrating every level of existence, the vicious slave master attempted to destroy all that made the Kidnapped African human.

The male was valued for the strength of his back and the power of his seed. The female was valued for her fertile womb and the lustful pleasures that could be taken at will. The family was destroyed by separating the men, women and children.

BUT, THE KIDNAPPED AFRICAN WOULD NOT DIE!

Then, the final indignity was inflicted upon the Kidnapped African. Rewriting this bloody saga of captivity and affliction, the ruthless slave master attempted to close the eyes and minds of his human property to the past and land from which they had been stolen in the night - hiding forever the greatest wrong ever committed by one people against another.

The pain and horror of the captivity were replaced by endless pages of silence and insincere apologies. The muffled screams of Black men hanging were drowned out by pompous speeches loudly proclaiming the American dream for all.

BUT, THE KIDNAPPED AFRICAN WOULD NOT DIE!

The faint remembrance of the African Homeland was deeply buried deep within their souls - deeper than the whip could reach - deeper than the hangman's noose - deep within the bosom of their God.

Mother Africa is now calling for her sons and daughters of the captivity to unite once more with the sons and daughters in her bosom, to begin again to build another dream that will never be destroyed.

The Kidnapped African who did not die, heeding the call of the eternal mother, is now set free to remake the universe in the image of good, in the image of God, in the image of the distant glory from whence they came.

FOR THE KIDNAPPED AFRICAN WOULD NOT DIE!

As far as many black Americans are concerned, the United States of America should be called what it is, what it has been, and—unless God intervenes to change the hearts, minds and spirits of all Americans— what it always will be: **"America the Racist."**

Chapter I

Book Overview

In this book, *America the Racist*, we will present a factually based analysis of the motives, attitudes, and treatment of black Americans by white Americans in power.

This book is a personal commentary on the social, political, and economic condition and experience of black Americans - African Americans - in America. It focuses on the root causes of these conditions, their present impact, and the future possibilities.

We will observe that the segregation and separation of black and white Christians in the practice of their religion undermines the *"one nation under God"* concept and fertilizes, nourishes, and perpetuates the seeds of division in America. These seeds of division grow into weeds of racism that undermine and devour the American Dream.

From before the birth of this nation in 1776, the powers that be in America have enslaved, abused, taken advantage of, and otherwise marginalized black Americans.

In spite of the fact that black men like Chrispus

Attucks died in the revolt and war against England, black Americans, free and slave, were totally marginalized by the white Christians who signed the Declaration of Independence, created the US Constitution, and otherwise founded this country.

We will show that the issue of slavery was an integral part of the evolution of this country, from its impact on the framing and adopting of the US Constitution, through the series of laws and court decisions that permitted, encouraged, and perpetuated the institution of slavery.

The *Making of A Slave*, as laid out in grim detail by Willie Lynch, an 18th Century authority on **Slavology** – was the process by which proud, productive kidnapped Africans were transformed into American Slaves.

The *Hundred Monkey Phenomenon*, a non-racial behavior modification process, provides: **when a finite number of a particular species have a certain thought or demonstrate a particular behavior, then all members of that species will become aware of that thought or will demonstrate that behavior.**

The *Slave Making Process* and the *Hundredth Monkey Phenomenon*

Interpreting the *Slave Making Process* in terms of the *Hundredth Monkey Phenomenon*, we see a scientific explanation for the plight of black Americans in the United States. Through the vicious, horrendous *Slave Making Process*, we will see that white Christian Americans created a *Slave Consciousness* or *Mentality* and a *Slave Master Consciousness or Mentality* that has impacted the thinking and behavior, to this very day, of both black and white Americans.

It is a fundamental principle of psychology that once a behavior is created, it will continue essentially unchanged until a new or different behavior is introduced and adopted.

We will also find that there have been no serious or sustained changes to the *Slave Consciousness and Slave Behaviors* so created by white Christian Americans using chains, whips, violence, death, and threats of death on black Christian Americans.

In fact, we will see that every significant attempt by black Americans to change their condition for the better has been met with subtle, overt, and blatant opposition by the white Americans in power.

This opposition was crystallized by the Emancipation Proclamation, energized through United States Supreme Court decisions, implemented through laws passed in state and local governments—often justified with claims of *"states rights"*. It is perpetuated to this very day in the hearts, minds and psyches of black and white Christian Americans.

As we look at America's track record in dealing with black Americans, we see new versions of the same *Slave Making* lessons described by Willie Lynch and used with brutal effectiveness by white American slave masters throughout the United States.

White Americans have committed brutalities and atrocities against black Americans from the Reconstruction, through the Black Codes, the Colfax Massacre in Louisiana, the Supreme Court ruling in Plessy v. Ferguson, the Coup of 1898 in Wilmington North Carolina, Jim Crow Laws, the Atlanta Riots, the Tulsa Oklahoma Destruction of Black Wall Street, the Rosewood Massacre, the New York City Riots, the Tuskegee Syphilis Experiment, the Birmingham Bombing of the 1960's, and the present day systematic destruction

and mis-education of black American children, to name
a few.

The purpose of these brutalities and atrocities—
Behavior Modifications and Behavior Implantations—
was and still is to TEACH AND RETEACH BLACK
AMERICANS THEIR PROPER PLACE IN A
WHITEMAN'S COUNTRY *"the so-called land of the
free and home of the brave"*.

The Paradigm of Slavery

White America, over the last 400 years, has designed, created, and perpetuated the *Slave Mentality*
and *Slave Behavior* that afflicts black Americans, and
the *Slave Master Mentality* and *Slave Master Behavior*
that afflicts white Americans. Together, these two mentalities and behaviors constitute the **Paradigm of Slavery.**

In spite of brief moments of hope that America
will live up to the lofty promises of its Constitution,
such as the Civil Rights Movement and legislation of
the 1950's, 1960's, and 1970's, the *Paradigm of Slavery* is so deeply entrenched in the psyche of America
that most attempts at substantial change are eventually
undermined and neutralized.

On the surface, things may look better. You
will see black and white Americans sitting together in
public restaurants, or riding together on public trans-
portation. You see more and more interracial couples
on television and in the community—even in cities
where a black man would have been lynched 40 or 50
years ago for even speaking in a certain way to a white
women.

But underneath the surface, on the under-belly
of reality where the ugly, unpleasant truth resides, virtually nothing has been done to change the *Paradigm*

of Slavery.

Black Americans are still second-class citizens. Historically black American colleges are still under-funded. The unemployment rate for young black Americans is much higher than their white counter-parts. In the 25-29 age group, an estimated 11.9 percent of black men were in prison or jails, compared with 3.9 percent of Hispanic males and 1.7 percent of white males.(Greater Diversity News, 5/25/06 edition)

According to a recent study from the Justice Policy Institute (http://www.justicepolicy.org), after 20 years of harsh criminal justice policies, there are more black American men in prison or jail than in college.

By the year 2000, there were 791,600 black men in jail or prison as compared to 603,032 enrolled in colleges or universities. In 1980, before the prison boom, black men in college outnumbered black men in jail or prison by a margin of more than 3 to 1. (See also 8/30/2002 article http://stopthedrugwar.org)

Yet, rather than change the *Paradigm of Slavery* and finally cleanse America of its sins and histori-cal crimes against humanity—the creation and per-petuation of slavery of black Americans—white Amer-ica wants to blame black Americans for their condition.

This *blame the victim* consciousness grows stronger each day in America as social, economic, and educational programs supported by well-intentioned white and black Christian Americans are reduced, un-dermined, and essentially eliminated.

The **Paradigm of Slavery** was and still is the creation of white Christian Americans. It has consumed the United States of America from its creation in 1776 to the present.

This destructive *Paradigm of Slavery* can only be changed by the white Christian Americans who maintain it, or are the beneficiaries of it, working together with the black Americans who continue to suffer under it.

The Solution: A Paradigm of Freedom

Finally, what is the solution? How do white and black Americans solve once and for all the issue of *Racism in America?*

First, we must realize that the problem cannot be solved on the same level of consciousness that created it in the first place. The *Paradigm of Slavery* can only be changed when a new lesson, a new consciousness—a *Paradigm of Freedom*—based on love, equality, and justice is burned indelibly into the mental, emotional, and spiritual psyche of each and every American. There must be a mutual acknowledgement of each person's humanity and a total commitment to the Golden Rule – *Do unto others, as you would have them do unto you.*

White America must confess its sins against black Americans. Each and every white person must take personal responsibility for the *Paradigm of Slavery* that was created in the past and perpetuated in the present. The spiritual problem of the *Slave Paradigm* cannot be resolved as long as white Americans continue to avoid personal responsibility by claiming that they did not personally participate in the slavery process and that no one is to blame since the people who personally inflicted slavery upon black Americans are all dead.

Black Americans must acknowledge that the *Paradigm of Slavery* has impacted them on every level of their lives. They must actively search out, confront, and replace all *Slave Mentalities* and *Behaviors* with new thoughts and behaviors consistent with being free, responsible, self-actualized human beings.

Why must the *Paradigm of Slavery* be resolved?

The bigger, more significant question is: *"Why must the Paradigm of Slavery be resolved?"*

The *Paradigm of Slavery* must be resolved if America is to survive and thrive on a long-term basis. When Abraham Lincoln said, *"a house divided against itself cannot stand"*, he was referring to different positions that states were taking on the issue of actual slavery.

Today, the house—America—is still divided against itself. The division now is a spiritual one. A country that does not live up to its creed is spiritually divided between the lofty God filled representations made in the United States Constitution, and the true state of affairs and consciousness that exists in reality.

Spiritually, the *Paradigm of Slavery* must be resolved if America is ever to achieve true and lasting peace and joy—*the kingdom of heaven*. This *Paradigm* must be resolved on a personal, individual basis—just as Slavery was created on a personal, individual basis.

Let us go to the scriptures to get a better understanding of why America must resolve the *Paradigm of Slavery*.

"The earth is the Lord's, and the fullness thereof; the world, and they that dwell therein."

"For he that founded it upon the seas, and established it upon the floods."

"Who shall ascend into the hill of the Lord? Or who shall stand in his holy place?"

"He that hath clean hands, and a pure heart; who hath not lifted up his soul unto vanity, nor sworn deceitfully."

> *"He shall receive the blessing from the*
> *Lord, and righteousness from the God of his*
> *salvation."*
>
> —*(*Psalm 24: 1-5)

The nation of America—the United States of America—did not enslave black Americans. America, in the determined grip of practicing slavery, did not whip, torture, rape, and maliciously kill black Americans.

Individual white Americans, most of them Christians, inflicted the pain and horror of slavery on individual black Americans. Individual black American women were raped, sodomized, and subjected to ungodly sexual lusts and fantasies of individual white men that would shame even the worst in ancient Babylon, or Sodom and Gomorrah.

Who is to blame?

We must now ask: **"How can white Christians today be responsible for, or impacted by, the sins and transgressions committed by their forefathers who created and constructed the *Paradigm of Slavery*?"**

White Americans consistently deny personal responsibility for the *Paradigm of Slavery* proclaiming that they did not enslave anyone. They deny personal responsibility for the practices and institution of slavery since those who created it are long dead and buried.

Let us again go to the Scriptures.

> "And God spake all these words, saying,
>
> *"I am the Lord thy God, which have*

brought thee out of the land of Egypt, out of the house of bondage."

"Thou shalt not make unto thee any graven image, or any likeness of any thing that is in the heaven above, or that is in the earth beneath, or that is in the water under the earth:"

"Thou shalt not bow down thyself to them, nor serve them: for I the Lord thy God am a jealous God, visiting the iniquity of the fathers upon the children unto the third and fourth generation of them that hate me:"

"And shewing mercy unto thousands of them that love me, and keep my commandments."

—(Exodus 20: 1–6)

This scripture implies that if individuals commit terrible acts that demonstrate a *Hatred for God*, then the punishment for these terrible acts can be inflicted upon future generations of these perpetrating individuals.

How does one *hate God?*

One hates God by disobeying the Commandments of God. When Jesus was asked at Matthew 22:36,

"Master, which is the great commandment in the law?"

Jesus replied at 22:37-40,

"Jesus said unto him, THOU SHALT LOVE THE LORD THY GOD WITH ALL THY HEART, AND WITH ALL THY SOUL, AND WITH ALL THY MIND."

"This is the first and great command-

ment."

*"And the second is like unto it, THOU
SHALT LOVE THY NEIGHBOUR AS THY-
SELF."*

*"On these two commandments hang
all the law and the prophets."*

Thus, based on the words of Jesus and the principle set forth in Genesis, **one demonstrates their hatred or contempt for God by treating their fellow
man—their neighbor—in a manner that they themselves would not like to be treated.**

No man desires to be treated like a slave. And
surely, NO WHITE CHRISTIAN MAN in America
during the days of actual slavery before the Civil War,
and afterwards, during the days of de facto slavery,
wanted to be treated in the manner that black Americans were treated.

Frederick Douglas, in response to some white
man's suggestion that slavery wasn't that bad, invited
that white man to spend one day as a slave and see if
his opinion wouldn't change.

The Filthiness of Slavery

Let us look again to the Scripture to get an understanding of a generation of white Christian Americans who self-righteously deny any culpability for the
Paradigm of Slavery.

*"There is a generation that are pure in
their own eyes, and yet is not washed from
their filthiness."*

*"There is a generation, O how lofty
are their eyes! And their eyelids are lifted
up."*

*"There is a generation, whose teeth
are as swords, and their jaw teeth as knives,
to devour the poor from off the earth, and the
needy from among men."*
—(Proverbs 30:12-14)

In America today, at the beginning of the 21st Century, there is a generation of white Christians *that are pure in their own eye, and yet not washed from their filthiness.* The filthiness that afflicts white America is the *filthiness of slavery*—of the *Paradigm of Slavery.*

The rich get richer and the poor get poorer

When we follow the trend of current events in America since the year 2000 and earlier, we see a determined assault on the poor, sick, mentally ill, and needy Americans of every variety. Poor Americans, black and white, find themselves getting poorer, while jobs are being exported to other countries, illegal immigrants are taking jobs at lower pay, and welfare safety nets disappear.

In America today, those in power— predominantly white Christian men—who control the government are truly *lofty in their own eyes. Their eyelids are lifted up* to their God, the unholy trinity— **Profit, Power, and Pleasure.**

Note: The American government is controlled by the President, the United States Senate, the United States House of Representatives, and the United States Supreme Court. Presently there are 100 United States Senators, 435 United States Representatives, 9 Supreme Court Justices, one President, and one Vice President.

In the history of America, from 1776 to 2005, a period of 229 years, there has never been an African American President or Vice President. There have been two black American Supreme Court Justices: Thurgood Marshall and Clarence Thomas in 229 years.

Five (5) black American US Senators

In 229 years, there have only been 5 black United States Senators. They were:

Hiram R. Revels: 1870-1871
Blanche K. Bruce: 1875-1881
Edward W. Brooke: 1967-1979
Carol Moseley-Braun: 1993-1999
Barack Obama: 2005 –2011

In 2005, there were 42 black Americans in the United States House of Representatives out of a total of 435 Representatives.

When you follow the current events in America —as highlighted by the treatment of Black Americans during Hurricane Katrina—you will see that the white Christians in power care little about the plight of poor black Americans. And yet, these same poor black Americans are the end product and resulting creation of the *Paradigm of Slavery* created and maintained by white Christian Americans.

As the bible predicts, and reality confirms, the white Christians in power in America today are doing every thing in their power to *"devour the poor from off the earth, and the needy from among men."*

The message is clear. By portraying the poor as lazy, shiftless black Americans who are out to get something for nothing, white Christians feel no re-morse in cutting welfare and health care benefits for the poor, while stuffing their own pockets with the corrupt fruits of outrageous corporate profits. Those who control the government cry out like *chicken little* that the sky is falling. They say that there is no money or resources to feed the hungry, to educate the children, to provide decent housing, to rehabilitate the prisoners, to guarantee America's promise of those inalienable rights of life, liberty and the pursuit of happiness.

An yet there is always money and resources to give big business a subsidy, to build a 200 million dollar *bridge to nowhere*, to fight an unnecessary war in a distant land, or to give tax breaks to people who don't need the money—who have all the money they could reasonably need in ten lifetimes.

What does this callous attitude toward black Americans and the poor in general do to the spiritual Soul of America?

Let us once again go to the Scriptures. In the 25th Chapter of Matthew where Jesus was describing a day of judgment, he said at verses 32-46:

> *"And before him shall be gathered all nations: and he shall separate them one from another, as a shepherd divideth his sheep from the goats:"*
> *"And he shall set the sheep on his right hand, but the goats on the left."*
> *"Then shall the King say unto them on his right hand, Come, ye blessed of my Father, inherit the kingdom prepared for you from the foundation of the world:"*
> *"For I was an hungred, and ye gave me meat: I was thirsty, and ye gave me drink: I was a stranger, ye took me in:"*
> *"Naked, and ye clothed me: I was sick, and ye visited me: I was in prison, and ye*

came unto me."

"Then shall **the righteous** *answer him, saying, Lord, when saw we thee an hungred, and fed thee? Or thirsty, and gave thee drink?"*

"When saw we thee a stranger and took thee in? or naked, and clothed thee?"

"Or when saw we thee sick, or in prison, and came unto thee?

*"And the King shall answer and say unto them, Verily I say unto you***, Inasmuch as ye have done it unto one of the least of these my brethren, ye have done it unto me.*"*

"Then **shall he say also unto them on the left hand***, Depart from me, ye cursed, into everlasting fire, prepared for the devil and his angels:"*

"For I was an hungred, and ye gave me no meat: I was thirsty, and ye gave me no drink:"

"I was a stranger, and ye took me not in: naked, and ye clothed me not: sick, and in prison, and ye visited me not."

"Then shall they also answer him saying, Lord, when saw we thee an hungred, or athirst, or a stranger, or naked, or sick, or in prison, and did not minister unto thee?"

*"Then shall he answer them, saying Verily I say unto you***, Inasmuch as ye did it not to one of the least of these, ye did it not to me.*"*

"And these shall go away into everlasting punishment: but the righteous into life eternal."

— (Matthew 25: 32-46)

Back to the Paradigm of Slavery

The Bible and the words of Jesus make it abundantly clear: the vile and vicious acts committed by white Christian Americans who practiced and enjoyed the benefits of the slavery of black Americans—who committed terrible acts of brutality and shame against *the least of them*—have sealed the fate of America.

Thus, based on the Bible and Christian theology that black and white American Christians profess to believe; on that great Judgment Day, when Jesus sits *upon the throne of his glory* separating the nations *one from another,* America will show itself to be spiritually bankrupt and *"Shall go away into the everlasting punishment... prepared for the devil and his angels."*

The great black American leader, Rev. Dr. Martin Luther King, Jr., recipient of the coveted Nobel Peace Prize, spoke eloquently about the shortcomings of America in his *"I Have a Dream"* speech delivered on the steps of the Lincoln Memorial at the 1963 March on Washington. Dr. King used impactful images describing the way America has treated the *least of them,* saying:

> *"...In a sense we have come to our nation's capital to cash a check. When the architects of our republic wrote the magnificent words of the Constitution and the Declaration of Independence, they were signing a promissory note to which every American was to fall heir. This note was a promise that all men, yes, black men as well as white men, would be guaranteed the unalienable rights of life, liberty, and the pursuit of happiness.*
>
> *It is obvious today that America has defaulted on this promissory note insofar as*

her citizens of color are concerned. Instead of honoring this sacred obligation, America has given the Negro people a bad check, a check which has come back marked "insufficient funds." But we refuse to believe that the bank of justice is bankrupt. We refuse to believe that there are insufficient funds in the great vaults of opportunity of this nation.

So we have come to cash this check —a check that will give us upon demand the riches of freedom and the security of justice. We have also come to this hallowed spot to remind America of the fierce urgency of now. This is no time to engage in the luxury of cooling off or to take the tranquilizing drug of gradualism. Now is the time to make real the promises of democracy. Now is the time to rise from the dark and desolate valley of segregation to the sunlit path of racial justice. Now is the time to lift our nation from the quick sands of racial injustice to the solid rock of brotherhood.

Now is the time to make justice a reality for all of God's children…"

And now the answer to the question, **"Why must America resolve the *Paradigm of Slavery*?"**, is obvious.

The *Paradigm of Slavery* **must be resolved if America is to avoid the judgment of *everlasting punishment reserved for the devil and his angels* because of how she has treated the *least of them* –** black Americans, slaves and free.

Changing the Fate of America

Is America doomed to the fate of arrogant, haughty, self-righteous nations that are built upon lies, deception, and injustice?

Will America continue to be like the *foolish man* referred to by Jesus in the *Sermon on the Mount* at Matthew 7: 26,27:

> *"And every one that heareth these sayings of mine, and doeth them not, shall be likened unto a foolish man, which built his house upon the sand:"*
> *"And the rain descended, and the floods come, and the winds blew, and beat upon that house; and it fell: and great was the fall of it"*
> —(Matthew 7: 26,27)

What about today: where do we stand in America in the 21st Century?

Today, at the beginning of the 21st Century, when the white Men in power—the United States Government—are bringing war to establish truth, justice, and the democratic American way into the Middle East, you would be EXTREMELY HARDPRESSED to find a WHITE CHRISTIAN MAN willing to exchange places with a black American.

You surely would not find a WHITE CHRISTIAN MAN, rich or poor, who would tolerate and accept the way black Americans are treated. The aftermath of Hurricane Katrina validates and underscores this point.

Chris Rock, a famous African American comedian, once joked that a white man sleeping in alley behind Carnegie Hall wouldn't change places with a black man—even a rich one.

Defending Slavery

Some white American Christians who owned slaves and practiced slavery justified their treatment of their slaves by alleging that slaves were some type of sub-human animal. Even in the US Constitution, slaves were counted as only three-fifths of a white person.

Following this reasoning, white American Christians could resolve the spiritual contradiction of "THOU SHALT LOVE THY NEIGHBOUR AS THY-SELF" with the way they treated slaves. Since the slaves were sub-human animals, this Golden Rule would not apply.

On the other hand however, many of these same white Christian Men, some of whom signed the Declaration of Independence and the Constitution of the United States, had sex with their captive black American female slaves who bore them many children.

The great variety of colors in the skin complexions of black Americans is a testament to the sexual pleasures the white Christian slave masters enjoyed in these mid-night encounters with their captive female slaves.

The Contradiction

If white Christian Americans justified their participation in the *Slavery Experience* by claiming that slaves were some type of sub-human species—a beast, then the fact that these white Christian slave masters had sex with their female slaves leads to one profound conclusion: white Christian men who had sexual intercourse with their female slaves would be guilty of *"laying with a beast."*

According to Exodus 22:19

"Whosoever lieth with a beast shall surely be put to death."

To commit an act that, under the Laws of God, would cause a man to be put to death, would surely be a demonstration of a *hatred and contempt* for God resulting in *"visiting the iniquity of the fathers upon the children unto the third and fourth generation…"*

On the other hand, if we assume that the black American slaves were indeed human beings, then those white Christian slave masters, who were married presumably to a white woman, would be guilty of adultery when they had sexual intercourse with their black female slaves.

Adultery is covered by one of the Ten Commandments.

Exodus 20:14,

"Thou shalt not commit adultery."

These adulterous sexual encounters committed by the white Christian slave master, in violation of the Ten Commandments would surely demonstrate a *hatred and disrespect* for God that would also impact future generations.

Conclusion

These unresolved spiritual issues that grow out the *Paradigm of Slavery,* unless they are properly addressed, will undermine the future existence of America on the world stage.

The Solution

The solution is found in the basic Christian Principle of confessing ones sins, seeking forgiveness, and making atonement.

**The spiritual process needed to save America
is clearly set forth at Numbers 5:7**

> *"Then they shall confess their sin
> which they have done: and he shall recom-
> pense his trespass with the principal thereof,
> and add unto it the fifth part thereof, and give
> it unto him against whom he hath trespassed."*

And also at James 5:16, the message is clear:

> *"Confess your faults one to another,
> and pray one for another, that ye may be
> healed."*

The Redemption Formula

If America is spiritually bankrupt today, because the sins and filthiness of slavery committed by
white Christians in the past have been visited unto the
present generation, then the way to remove this sin and
filthiness is:

1. The present generation of white Christian
   Americans must acknowledge and confess
   the sins and filthiness of their forefathers.
2. They must ask forgiveness from black
   Americans.
3. They must make atonement. Black and
   white Americans must pray one for another
   to be healed and made whole.

When this Redemption Formula is followed and
fulfilled by a certain number of black and white individual Christian Americans, the *Hundredth Monkey*

Phenomenon will work for **Good** in creating the ***Paradigm of Freedom,*** just as effectively it has worked for **Evil** in creating the ***Paradigm of Slavery.***

The *Paradigm of Freedom* so established, America can finally realize its promise, *"that all men are created equal, endowed by their Creator with certain unalienable Rights, that among these are Life, Liberty and the pursuit of Happiness."*

America can then live by the Golden Rule for all its citizens and fulfill its destiny as described at Deuteronomy 7: 9:

> *"**Know therefore that the Lord thy God, he is God, the faithful God which keepeth covenant and mercy with them that love him and keep his commandments to a thousand generations;"***

Chapter II

Observations and Commentaries

The impact of the *Paradigm of Slavery* has touched every facet of life in America. Below are a few observations and commentaries on ways this *Paradigm* has influenced the lives of black and white Americans.

One nation under God

If America represents itself as *"one nation under God"*, then based on the way black Americans and poor Americans of all races are treated, that *God* must be the ***Unholy Trinity – Profit, Power, and Pleasure.***

Nazi soldiers treated better than black American soldiers.

Aging black American soldiers tell stories of rampart racism in the United States during and after the Second World War. When German Nazi soldiers were captured and transported on trains to prisoner-of-war camps in the southern United States, the captured Germans could eat in the segregated dining cars, while their black American military guards could not. In America, a white German Nazi prisoner was given more respect than a black American soldier.

Black American police officers could not arrest white Americans.

As integration began to take hold in the 1960's throughout the southern United States, police departments that had for over 100 years been exclusively a white man's job, were faced with many dilemmas.

How would black police officers be able to function along side white police officers, many of whom had clubbed, put dogs on, shot and otherwise abused black Americans in the not-too-distant past?

Black police officers that first integrated southern police departments had limited arrest powers. For example, black policemen tell stories of how they could only arrest black people, but could not arrest white people. I guess, in those days, if a white person committed a crime in front of a black police officer, all that the black officer could do was call in and tell a white officer what he had seen. Chances are, if the black police officer was the only witness to the crime—tried before a white jury—the white perpetrator would be found not guilty.

Racist treatment of black police officers took place in the northern states also.

Black police officers in Philadelphia could not ride together in a patrol car.

A retired Philadelphia police officer told about the LWW policy in the police department. LWW means *"Love White Women"*. There was an unwritten rule in the Philadelphia police department that two black police officers could not ride in the same patrol car. It was perfectly fine that two white police officers could ride together in a patrol car. Even a white and black policeman could share a patrol car. Why was it unacceptable for two black police officers to ride together?

The reason was LWW. The Philadelphia police brass evidently believed that if two black police officers rode together in a patrol car, sooner of later, they would encounter a white woman. Since, as many white men believe, black men *"Love White Women"*, the thought of two black police officers – with guns – approaching a white woman who was driving or walking recklessly, could only lead to one thing – *rape and mayhem in the first degree.*

Thus, to prevent this *unacceptable situation* from ever happening to a white woman, two black police officers could not ride together in a patrol car in the city of Philadelphia, Pennsylvania. All because of the LWW policy.

West Indians are different from black Americans born in America.

Black Americans, born and raised in America, especially for many generations are different from West Indians, Carribeans, and other people of color who don't share the American slave ancestry.

Although black Americans and other blacks who were born and raised outside of the United States may look alike on the outside, they are totally different on the inside—in their psyche—in their mentality.

In contemporary America—*today*—at the beginning of the 21st Century, if you go to any city that has a significant number of West Indians or black Americans of West Indian descent, you will find that these West Indians, or black Americans of West Indian descent, will own more businesses, have better jobs, be more involved politically, and generally be more prosperous than many native born black Americans who have been in this country for generations.

Let us consider some examples:

Marcus Garvey, black charismatic leader of the early 20th Century, had millions of followers in America. He probably had the greatest following of black Americans of any black leader in the first half of the 20th Century. Garvey was from Jamaica West Indies.

Even the world respected Colin Powell, the only black American to head the Joint Chiefs of Staff and the first black American to be Secretary of State, is of West Indian heritage.

When you consider black businesses that flourished in Harlem, New York City in the 1920's through the 1950's, a vast majority were owned by black Americans of West Indian descent. Even today, at the beginning of the 21st Century, there are more businesses owned and operated by black West Indians or black Americans of West Indian descent operating in Brooklyn New York, than there are businesses owned or operated by "native"—bred out of the bowels of American slavery—black Americans in the entire city of New York, and probably in the entire state of New York.

If you travel throughout the United States of America, north, south, east and west, you will probably find greater advances in businesses and even the job market by black Americans of West Indian descent than by *"native"* black Americans.

An example of this extraordinary presence of black West Indians and Africans can be found in the education and management staff at Historically Black Colleges throughout America.

Black people and black Americans who have come to America from the West Indies, or in fact from anywhere outside of America, tend to do better, own more businesses, acquire more wealth and power, than *"native"* black Americans who were born and raised in America of parents who were born and raised under the American *Paradigm of Slavery*.

For discussion purposes, I shall label *"native"* black Americans as black Americans who were born in America of parents who were the descendents—going back at least four generations—of American slaves and free blacks who coexisted in America.

"Foreign born" blacks are black people, including black Americans, who were either born and raised outside of America, or whose parents were born and raised outside of America. The most predominant *"foreign born"* blacks were initially black people from the West Indies or the Caribbean, but now includes all black people from anywhere outside of America.

The primary difference between *"native"* and *"foreign"* black Americans lies in the **residual effects of the Paradigm of Slavery** inflicted by white Americans on black Americans from the birth of the United States to the present.

The white American slave masters taught black slaves specifically, and black Americans in general, how to be slaves and nothing else. Virtually nothing has been done to date by white Christian Americans to undue the damage they have done to black Americans for the last 400 years.

Maintaining the Illusion of White Superiority

In order to maintain the illusion of white superiority over black Americans, white Americans systematically kept talented black Americans from competing on every level.

Sports

White Americans have systematically kept black American atheletes from competing in the sports arena so that white atheletes could always appear to be the best in their particular sport.

Let's consider professional boxing. For many years after the end of the Civil War, black boxers were not permitted to box white boxers. The implication was that a black man was not skilled or intelligent enough to defeat a white boxer. In addition, there was a feeling in America that giving a black American a chance at the heavyweight title would be too costly and might offset the *"moral balance"* of American society.

The way to insure this myth of white superiority was to bar black boxers from participating in title fights. In reality, many black boxers were far superior to white boxers, but were never given the chance to compete.

The racism was so strong in America that a black boxer could not even fight a white boxer on American soil. Jim Jeffries, white heavyweight champion in the early 1900's refused to fight famous American fighter Jack Johnson (1878 – 1946) because be was black.

White America could not stomach the thought, vision and symbolism of a black man physically beating a white man and drawing blood. This symbolism was at total odds with the *Paradigm of Slavery.*

To get a title fight, Jack Johnson, had to go to Sydney, Australia to fight Tommy Burns, the Canadian heavyweight champion in 1908.

Johnson defeated Burns and became the world heavyweight champion. America refused to recognize Jack Johnson as heavyweight champion and there began a desperate search for a Great White Hope to whip this black man and put him back in his place as a second-rate, inferior boxer who was no match for a skillful white boxer. In addition to the vindication of white manhood—*Follow the Money*—a lot of money could be made on a fight to teach this black American his place in life.

Jack Johnson became the official *Heavyweight Champion of the World* on July 4, 1910 in Las Vegas, Nevada when he defeated Jim Jeffries, retired white heavyweight champion. Jeffries was the first of many *"Great White Hopes"*.

Johnson's victory over the *"Great White Hope"* sparked race riots and violence against black Americans by angry white Americans. The Texas State Legislature banned films showing Jack Johnson's victories over white boxers for fear of causing more riots and violence.

Not only did Jack Johnson whip white boxers, he committed the *"Capital Sin"* of **marrying a white woman.** In 1912, when interracial marriages were illegal in most states in American, Jack Johnson was convicted under the Mann Act of transporting his wife across state lines and sentenced to a year in prison.

To avoid jail, Johnson fled the country and lived in Canada and Europe for seven years. In 1920 he returned to America and served his sentence. White America had done in the courts what the *"Great White Hopes"* could not do in the ring—beat a black American man down and get its *pound of flesh.*

This proud black American champion boxer that white America portrayed as an ignorant brute was in fact quite intelligent and also an inventor. In 1922 Jack Johnson, the first black American heavyweight champion, patented improvements to the wrench (U.S. Patent# 1,413,121).

Baseball

From the time the sport of baseball—the *"Great American Pastime"*—was developed, for nearly 100 years, black American baseball players were not permitted to play in the professional baseball leagues with or against white baseball players. The white Americans who controlled the baseball leagues justified their racist discrimination against black American baseball players by perpetuating the idea that baseball was a game of thinking and skill. They claimed that black baseball players did not have the brains or skill to play in the *"white man's game"* of baseball.

For nearly 100 years white Christian Americans—the president of the United States, the Senators and Congressmen, Ministers and Priests, white people from virtually every station in life—saw no problem with this blatant racist discrimination against black Americans who wanted to play professional baseball.

In fact, shortly after the Civil War, the National Association of Base Ball Players passed a resolution that excluded *"any club which may be composed of one or more colored (black American) players."*

Octavius Catto, one of the pioneers of black American baseball, was murdered by a white man in 1871.

In the early 1900's, many black American baseball teams called themselves names such as the "Cuban Giants" and the "...Cuban Stars". These so-called *"Cuban Teams"* were all composed of black Americans. They call themselves *"Cuban"* to increase their acceptance by white Americans. To this day, white Americans tend to accept any nationality ahead of black Americans.

As a result of the financial success of the black

American baseball leagues, and with some political pressure to integrate baseball, Branch Rickey, Owner/ General Manager of the Brooklyn Dodgers, in 1947, gave Jackie Robinson the opportunity to play in the white man's game of baseball. Jackie Robinson became the first black American to play major league baseball.

The integration of baseball meant the end of the black baseball leagues as a commercial enterprise in the black American community.

Once in the game, black baseball players began to excel. Now, over 50 years after white America permitted black American baseball players to participate in the game, black players hold many of the world records.

Hank Aaron, a black American, took the home run record from the legendary Babe Ruth who had hit 714 home runs in his career. Hank Aaron's lifetime home run record of 755 home runs was surpassed by Barry Bonds, also a black American.

Once black baseball players got into the professional leagues, white Americans who control baseball then restricted the management of baseball teams to white men. White Americans in power, perpetuating racism, once more claimed that black men did not have the intelligence or skill to manage a baseball team.

Today, at the beginning of the 21st Century, there are a few black managers still fighting to overcome the existent racism in *"the Great American Pastime"*.

Football

Very similar to baseball, the white Americans who control football spent years keeping black American athletes from playing. Even after football was finally integrated, for another 20 to 25 years black athletes were restricted to certain positions. The quarterback position, for example, was considered off-limits to black football players. Again the reason given by the white Americans who control football was that black players did not have the intellect to quarterback a football team.

Although black quarterbacks had been excelling with black college football teams, when these players came to the pros, they were encouraged to change their positions to anything but quarterback.

White Americans in power resist black Americans performing in any capacity where they are required to tell white people what to do. There is a core resistance in America to white Americans taking orders from black Americans. Having a black American quarterback tell white American players what to do contradicts the *Paradigm of Slavery*.

Golf

For nearly 150 years through the early 1960's, white Americans excluded black Americans from playing professional golf. Of the more than 5,000 golf courses in the United States in 1939, fewer than 20 were open to black American golfers.

It is ironic that the golf tee used today is virtually the same as the wooden golf tee invented and patented in 1899 by Dr. George F. Grant, a black American golfer.

As usual, white Americans considered Golf to be a thinking man's game of skill that black Americans could not play. Tiger Woods has forever destroyed this myth.

Today, at the dawning of the 21st Century, there are still country clubs with golf courses that do not welcome black American golfers. These country clubs give great excuses for not having black American golfers playing on their courses. In reality, it is the operation of the *Paradigm of Slavery*. Often golf courses are the venues of choice for white businessmen to discuss business deals. This automatically excludes black businessmen from *"the Deal"*.

The Military

Segregation and discrimination against black Americans existed in the United States Military from the Civil War until 1948 when President Harry Truman issued an executive order abolishing segregation in the United States Armed Forces.

Public Schools in America

In 1954 the United States Supreme Court determined that separate-but-equal education of black Americans was not equal and not just. It was unconstitutional under Brown v. The Board of Education. Once the Supreme Court had spoken, white school districts throughout the south fought the implementation of this legitimate order of America's highest court.

After many black Americans sued the white public school systems to force them to implement the desegregation order of the Supreme Court, the white people in control of the schools reluctantly complied.

The dilemma that confronted black Americans when the public schools were desegregated was that the school systems were still under the control of the same white Americans who had to be forced to integrate in the first place.

The white Americans in power were still in charge. These same white people were charged with overseeing and implementing the school desegregation plan. Their racist, slave master consciousness was not changed by court orders to integrate the public schools. To a major extent, the hearts, minds, spirits, and psyches of the white Americans in charge of school desegregation were basically the same as they had been during the period of segregation. The racist, slave master mentality was too deeply ingrained in the consciousness of the white Americans in charge and white America in general.

As a result, the slave master consciousness permeated every aspect of school desegregation. Schools that had served black American students prior to integration were generally shut down, abandoned, and often demolished. Black students were bused to schools that, prior to desegregation, had only served white students. The subtle implication was that the black public schools were inferior and not worthy of having white students attend.

What about discipline?

Prior to school desegregation, white schools and black schools used corporeal punishment (spanking etc.) usually in elementary and middle schools, when students were between 5 and 12 years old. In many schools systems, corporeal punishment was generally endorsed prior to school desegregation.

Once the public schools were integrated, corporeal punishment began to disappear. Once again, the vision of a black American teacher spanking white American children was contrary to the *Paradigm of Slavery.*

White teachers paid more than black teachers.

One reason that white Americans resisted integration so violently was that, in public school systems throughout the south, white teachers were generally paid more than black teachers of comparable experience and education.

In North Carolina, for example, interviews with retired black teachers who had worked in the public school system before and after integration, revealed that, during the period of segregation, black teachers and school administrators were paid at least 20% to 35% less than white teachers with comparable education and experience.

This disparity in teacher pay again demonstrated that the separate-but-equal doctrine—legitimatized in 1896 by the United States Supreme Court in Plessy v. Ferguson—was in reality a legal cover for the disparate, unequal, and unjust treatment of black Americans on every level of American life.

The real tragedy of this unjust situation was that once integration took place in North Carolina, the white American powers that controlled the state government did not immediately rectify the unfair difference between the salaries of black and white teachers.

Instead of immediate action the North Carolina state government adjusted the black teachers salaries gradually over a period of at least three years.

Can you imagine how black American teachers must have felt working side-by-side with white American teachers, knowing that the white teacher is being paid more, simply because he or she was white.

Knowing that black teachers were paying the same if not more for food, clothing, shelter, and other necessities of life than the white teachers, what moral justification could there be for continuing this salary inequity for three and possibly more years?

Where was the love of the white Christians in power for their fellow man?

Had they again forgotten the Golden Rule?

They were trapped in the confines of the *Paradigm of Slavery*.

Chapter III

American Religion

How does America practice its religion?

If America is truly *"One nation under God"*, let us look at how America practices its religion and worships its God.

The separation and segregation that exists in America today starts in the Churches of America. From 11:00am to 12 noon on Sunday morning is the most segregated and separated hour in America. This is the hour that most American Christians worship their God.

It was this way in 1776 when the nation was founded; it was this way in 1863 when President Abraham Lincoln issued the Emancipation Proclamation; it was this way when John F. Kennedy was president and the so-called Great Society was born; it was this way when Hurricane Katrina struck New Orleans; IT IS THIS WAY NOW AS YOU READ THIS BOOK.

If you could visit 1,000 churches on any given Sunday morning, you would find that the vast majority of churches are segregated – black Americans attend churches where virtually all members are black, and white Americans attend churches where virtually all members are white. At least 95% - 950 churches would be totally segregated – either all white or all black. Only 5% or less would be churches where the membership is racially integrated to any significant degree.

The words of Edmund Burke, over 200 years ago gives us a unique insight into the relationship between the way one's religion is practiced and the way one's government operates.

"True religion is the foundation of society, the basis on which all true civil government rests, and from which power derives its authority, laws their efficacy, and both their sanction. If it is once shaken by contempt, the whole fabric cannot be stable or lasting."

—(Edmund Burke (1729-1797), English orator and statesman.)

The segregation and separation that is perpetrated and perpetuated by the manner in which religion is practiced in America forms the basis on which our government rests. Religion is the spiritual foundation of American government.

As long as white and black Americans are divided in the practice of their religion, the American government will be divided in the execution of its authority and laws.

Let us consider why this separation of the races is so basic in the practice of religion in America.

What Color is God?

If we consider *Genesis 1: 26, 27*, we will gain a perspective on the racial separation that exist in American churches.

> *"And God said, Let us make man in*
> *our image, after our likeness: and let them*
> *have dominion over the fish of the sea, and*
> *over the fowl of the air, and over the cattle,*
> *and over all the earth, and over every creep-*
> *ing thing that creepeth upon the earth."*
> *"So God created man in his own im-*
> *age, in the image of God created he him; male*
> *and female created he them."*
>   —(Genesis 1:26, 27)

Based on the above Biblical passage, it is understandable that a white Christian American would
see God, or the God image, as a white man. This imagery is further confirmed by the depiction of *Jesus,*
the only Son of God, as a blond-haired, blued-eyed
white man.

Visit any white Christian church in America
that has a depiction of God, Jesus, or any of the hallowed saints. You will find images of white men or
white women. If one visited every white Christian
church in America—today, in the 21st Century—there
is <u>virtually no possibility</u> that you will find the depiction of any of the biblical figures as black people.

In America, white Christians have indeed put a
face and color on God, Jesus, and the saints. That color
is white and that face is Caucasian.

It is probably this so-called *special kinship* and
claimed lineage with a white God that many white
Americans use as justification to *have dominion over*
black Americans. Indeed, when a white Christian minister was justifying the killing of black Americans in
the coup of 1898 in Wilmington, North Carolina, he
stated:

*"Here, the ruling motive is the outraged dig-
nity of a proud <u>dominant race</u> calmly determined to assert its<u> innate right to rule</u> ..."*

Don't touch my blue-eyed Jesus

Let us test and validate this observation. Suppose there was a white minister of a typical white
Christian church in America with a great depiction of
the crucifixion hung above the alter showing a white,
blond, blue-eyed Jesus nailed to the cross. One day this
white Christian minister heard about the Black
Madonna worshiped in some European countries and
decided that if the Madonna was black, then Jesus must
have been black.

The concept of a non-white Jesus is set forth in
Revelation 1:13-15,

*"And in the midst of the seven candlesticks
one like unto the Son of man, clothed with a
garment down to the foot, and girt about the
paps with a golden girdle."*
*"His head and his hairs were white like wool,
as white as snow and his eyes were as a flame
of fire;"*
*"And his feet like unto fine brass, as if they
burned in a furnace; and his voice as the
sound of many waters."*
               —(Revelation 1:13-15)

Excited about his new revelation, the white
minister removed the original crucifixion depiction and
replaced with an identical picture except that Jesus was
shown as a black man. On the following Sunday, the
excited minister shared his new revelation that Jesus
was a black man and pointed proudly up to the new

depiction of Jesus' crucifixion.

I can tell you with absolute certainty that before the sun goes down that fateful Sunday, the excited white Christian minister would be looking for a new church, the blond, blue-eyed Jesus would be back above the pulpit, and the black Jesus depiction would be burning on the trash pile.

This is all understandable from a white American's perspective. However, I can remember hearing of a prominent black Christian minister who learned about the Black Madonna. He reasoned further that Israel is really in North Africa, and that there was scripture that described Jesus with woolly hair and burnished bronze feet.

Excited about his newly discovered understanding, the black Christian minister had the white, blond, blue-eyed Jesus that had been hanging above the alter for over 25 years, removed and replaced with an ethnically sensitive depiction of the crucifixion with a black Jesus on the cross.

The following Sunday, when the excited black minister shared his new understanding and pointed up to the black Jesus on the cross, the church elders were visibly unamused. Immediately after the service, the elders called a meeting with the black minister and advised him in no uncertain terms that: either he put their white Jesus on the cross back above the alter, or he would have an immediate opportunity to preach elsewhere. In other words, in the colorful language of black American church folks, *"let the door knob hit you where the good Lord split you."*

This acceptance by black Americans of a God and his only son Jesus that does not look like them was once the norm among black Christians. In the 1950's and even into the 1970's, depicting a black Jesus on the cross was a rarity in the black churches. Most black churches had some form of a white Jesus in their depictions of the crucifixion, on their church fans, and on their church programs.

Even today, in the 21st Century, when you visit black Christian churches in America, finding a black Jesus and saints in depictions of the crucifixion is still rare. What many black Christian churches have done is show an erected cross without a figure—white or black—at all.

White Christian churches today, in the 21st Century, show Jesus as white on their depictions of the crucifixion, on their fans, on their programs, and on their advertisements and literature.

One must ask: if God made man in his own image, and the generally accepted image of God and Jesus is that of a white man, "why would black Americans continue to worship a God and Jesus that does not look like them?" In fact, why would black Christians worship a God and his son Jesus that looks like the people that have oppressed, intimidated, brutalized and enslaved them?

On first glance this looks like the great contradiction. However, as we will see later in this book in the sections on the *Hundredth Monkey Phenomenon* and *The Making of a Slave*, this apparent contradiction is indeed the direct result of the *Paradigm of Slavery* inflicted by white Christian Americans on black Christian Americans.

This same identity confusion was established by Dr. Kenneth Clark in his psychological demonstration in the Doll Experiments that formed a part of the research basis for the 1954 Brown v. the Board of Education of Topeka, Kansas, et al. Supreme Court decision. This decision ruled that segregation in the public schools was unconstitutional.

The Doll Experiments

A series of experiments were developed and executed by black psychologists to demonstrate the psychological impact of the so-call separate-but-equal segregationist philosophy and experience that white Americans had inflicted upon black Americans, in particular black children.

Dr. Kenneth B. Clark and his wife Mamie Phipps Clark were a husband-and-wife team of African American psychologists who were well known for their 1940's experiments using dolls to study children's attitudes about race. These experiments grew out of Mamie Clark's master's degree thesis. Dr. Kenneth Clark was the first African American to receive a Ph.D. in psychology from Columbia University and his wife Dr. Mamie Clark was the second.)

Basically little black children were shown white dolls and black dolls. The black children were asked questions about the dolls such as:

1. Which doll was pretty?
   Black children chose the white dolls.
2. Which doll was ugly?
   Black children chose the black dolls.
3. Which doll was good?
   Black children chose the white dolls.
4. Which doll was bad?
   Black children chose the black dolls.

When the black children were asked which doll looked like them, it was immediately clear that there was a great deal of confusion in how the black children saw themselves based on the color model.

The Doll Experiments further show that black

children generally preferred to play with white dolls. When black children were asked to fill in human figures with the color of their skin, they colored themselves in a lighter shade than they actually were. Generally these black children viewed white as pretty and good and black as bad and ugly.

The results of these Doll Experiments was viewed as direct evidence of the effects of internalized racism caused by the stigmatization of segregation.

Drs. Kenneth and Mamie Clark testified as expert witnesses in several school desegregation cases in the 1950's. These cases were eventually combined into the landmark desegregation case, Brown v. Board of Education of Topeka, Kansas, et al., officially determining that segregation, separate-but-equal, violated the United States Constitution.

Applying the ramifications of the Doll Experiments to the practice of religion in black and white Christian churches, it is understandable why most black and virtually all white Christians have extreme difficulty accepting the image of a black Jesus, or a black God.

The profound impact of the *Slave Making Process* continues to manifest in black and white Christian Americans. The *Slave Mentality* and the *Slave Master Mentality* will continue to fuel the *Paradigm of Slavery* that consumes black and white Americans until it is replaced by a new consciousness, behavior and paradigm—one truly based on the principal of *doing unto others as you would have them do unto you.*

God and the Flag

Let us consider the words and images used in the *Pledge of Allegiance* to the Flag:

*"I pledge allegiance to the flag of the
United States of America, and to the republic
for which it stands, one nation under God,
indivisible, with liberty and justice for all."*

When Americans recite " ... *one nation under
God*", in the pledge, they are being duplicitous and deceitful because, as long as white and black Americans
are divided in the practice of their religion, there is no
"one nation under God".

As long as there is no *"one nation under God,"*
Americans are demonstrating contempt for the religious values that form the foundation of the government—that CANNOT BE STABLE OR LASTING.

American Churches Lead the Way

The separation and segregation that exists in the
churches of America permeates every segment of the
community and the society.

For example, in 1954, the United States Supreme Court determined that the discriminatory practice of racial segregation violated the 14th amendment
to the United States Constitution that guarantees all
citizens equal protection of the laws. This earth shaking
Supreme Court case ruled that the separate but equal
doctrine developed in the courts of the United States
after the Civil War was unconstitutional.

It was no longer legal for school systems
throughout the country to short change its black American children and citizens. Public school systems, supported with tax payer dollars of black and white Americans, could no longer pay black American teachers less
than white teachers; could no longer provide second-
hand, used, hand-me-down textbooks to black students;
could no longer force black American children to at-

tend rundown, dilapidated, hazardous buildings with outdoor toilets, while white students had higher paid teachers, new books, and shiny new facilities with indoor toilets and the latest in educational architecture.

When the 1954 Supreme Court decision made segregation unconstitutional and illegal, in many instances it then was the churches—the white American churches—that took the lead in undermining the spirit and letter of the law.

Many white Americans through their white churches—refusing to yield to or obey the law of the land—set up private Christian schools where white Christian children could attend and black Christian children could not attend. This practice of segregation in private schools continues to an extent to this day over 50 years after the United States Supreme Court decided that segregation was illegal.

This trend of setting up *"private church schools"* by white churches to avoid integration was so prevalent throughout the south that the Unitarian Universalist Association, one of the church organizations that supported integration, passed a General Resolution in 1970 providing:

WHEREAS, private schools are springing up in many parts of the country under church sponsorship with the aim of desegregation of public schools, thus subverting the Supreme Court order for immediate desegregation; and

WHEREAS, the Unitarian Universalist Association has repeatedly affirmed its stand for school integration and as recently as April, 1970, the Board of Trustees of the UUA expressed dismay at the continued resistance to school integration and has stood for the use public funds for public schools; and

WHEREAS, the new church – sponsored private schools are, in many cases, seeking state and federal aid:

NOW THEREFORE BE IT RE-SOLVED: That the Ninth General Assembly of the Unitarian Universalist Association deplores the development of segregated private church-related schools, and petitions the Department of Health, Education and Welfare and Office of Education to deny any federal funds to such schools, and further urges the Internal Revenue Service to deny granting income tax deductions for contributions to such schools.

Where Was The Love?

When the US Supreme Court determined that the public schools must desegregate, where was the love by many white Christians of their fellow man in this so called *"one nation under God"*? Where was the love of many white Christians for their fellow Christians—black American Christians? It was not there.

Is Every White American A Racist?

Is every white American a racist? No – not every white American is a racist. There were many white Americans, many white churches and religious organizations, and many white organizations that embraced integration as being long overdue.

However, many white Americans simply don't think about racism. They hide their heads in the sand of pious sanctimony until stark pictures of the suffering and neglect of black Americans stranded in the aftermath of Hurricane Katrina fill their television screens.

It is the same care, concern, and Christian love that many white Americans showed in the 1950's and 1960's when vicious dogs tore flesh off black Americans and billy clubs of racist white police officers cracked the skulls and bones of black Americans who were trying to integrate the public schools and obtain the life, liberty, and pursuit of happiness that the founding fathers had promised when America was created.

Attempting to explain this separation and segregation that exists in American churches today, white churches would say that it's not their fault. Black Christians would be welcome to worship with them. Black churches would say that white Christians are welcome to worship with them. Although Christians are supposed to love each other, the *Paradigm of Slavery*, until it is resolved, will keep black Christians and white Christians from ever worshipping together in any meaningful way.

> *"And I will kill her children with death; and all the churches shall know that I am he which searcheth the reins and hearts: and I will give unto every one you according to your works."*
>
> —(Revelation 2:23)

Historically, white Americans have undermined the progress of and attacked black Americans virtually every time they (black Americans) made economic, political, or artistic gains.

Chapter IV

America's Record in Dealing with Black Americans

The history of black America is filled with examples of white Christian Americans committing horrible and vicious acts against black Americans, from discrimination and injustice to intimidation and murder. The purpose and intent of these actions by white Americans was and still is to diminish, undermine, and deny to black Americans the rights, privileges and protections promised in the United States Constitution.

Let us consider a few of the horrible actions perpetrated on black Americans by some white Christian Americans:

The "Coup of 1898" in Wilmington, North Carolina

The "Coup of 1898" is perhaps the only instance in American history where a lawfully elected government was forcefully displaced by armed white Christians. In 1898, the black American citizens of the City of Wilmington, North Carolina were threatened, intimidated, run out of town, and killed by white Christians who wanted to re-establish the white supremacy they enjoyed prior to the U. S. Civil War.

I relate this event in great detail because the *Coup of 1898* signaled the end of Reconstruction and the beginning of the racist *Jim Crow* period in which black Americans were systematically excluded from participating in the great American democracy dominated and controlled by white Americans.

Black Americans were virtually prevented from voting, holding public office, working in certain jobs, participating in professional sports, owning certain businesses, receiving a first-rate education, and from otherwise enjoying the rights, privileges, and benefits promised in the United States Constitution.

These events in Wilmington, North Carolina were duplicated or simulated in towns, cities, and states throughout the South specifically, and throughout America in general.

This Coup of 1898 was a well-planned, organized insurrection conducted by white businessmen.

After the Civil War, Wilmington, North Carolina was a prosperous southern town in which black Americans had achieved a general level of political and economic success. Black Christian Americans and fair-minded white Christian Americans had worked together to establish a duly elected government and city where white and black Americans could live together in peace, harmony, and prosperity.

However, many of the white citizens were opposed to the life, liberty, and pursuit of happiness enjoyed by the black citizens in Wilmington. This dislike and disgust with the way things were in Wilmington was so intense that the Wilmington North Carolina Chamber of Commerce issued a *"White Declaration of Independence"* affirming and justifying their desire to deprive the black citizens of their constitutional rights.

The *White Declaration of Independence* provided as follows:

"THE WHITE DECLARATION OF INDEPENDENCE"

"Believing that the Constitution of the United States contemplated a government to be carried on by an enlightened people: believing that its framers did not anticipate the enfranchisement of an ignorant population of African origin, and believing that the men of the State of North Carolina who joined in forming the Union did not contemplate for their descendants a subjection to an inferior race;

We, the undersigned citizens of the city of Wilmington and county of New Hanover, do hereby declare that we will no longer be ruled, and will never again be ruled, by men of African origin. This condition we have in part endured because we felt that the consequences of the war of succession were such to deprive us of the fair consideration of many of our countrymen.

We believe that, after more than thirty years, this is no longer the case.

The stand we now pledge ourselves to is forced upon us suddenly by crisis, and our eyes are open to the fact that we must act now or leave our descendants to a fate too gloomy to be borne.

While we recognize the authority of the United States, and will yield to it if exerted, <u>we would not for a moment believe that it is the purpose of more than 60,000,000 of our own race to subject us permanently to a fate to which no Anglo-Saxon has ever been forced to submit</u>.

We, therefore, believing that we represent unequivocally the sentiment of white people of this county and city, hereby for ourselves, and representing them, proclaim:

That the time has passed for the intelligent citizens of this community, owning 95 percent of the property and paying taxes in like proportion, to be ruled by Negroes.

2. That we will not tolerate the action of unscrupulous white men in affiliating with Negroes so that by means of their votes they can dominate the intelligent and thrifty element in the community, thus causing business to stagnate and progress to be out of the question.

3. That the Negro has demonstrated, by antagonizing our interest in every way, and especially by his ballot, that he is incapable of realizing that his interest are and should be identical with those of the community.

4. That the progressive element in any community is the white population, and that the giving of nearly all of the employment to Negro laborers has been against the best interest of this county and city, and is sufficient reason why the city of Wilmington with its natural advantages has not become a city of at least 50,000 inhabitants.

5. That we propose in the future to give the white men a large part of the employment heretofore given to Negroes, because we realize that white families can not thrive here unless there are more opportunities for the different members of said family.

6. That the white men expect to live in this community peaceably, to have and provide absolute protection for their families, who shall be safe from insult from all persons whomsoever, We are prepared to treat the Negroes with justice and consideration in all matters which do not involve sacrifices of the interest of the intelligent and progressive portion of the community. But we are equally prepared now and immediately to enforce what we know to be our rights.

7. That we have been, in our desire for harmony and peace, blinded to our best interests and our rights. A climax was reached when the Negro paper of this city published an article so vile and slanderous that it would in most communities have resulted in lynching of the editor. We deprecate lynching, and yet there is no punishment provided by the laws adequate for this offense. We therefore owe it to the people of this community and of this city, as a protection against such license in the future, that the paper known as the Record cease to be published, and that its editor be banished from this community.

We demand that he leave this city within twenty-four hours after the issuance of this proclamation; second, that the printing press from which the Record has been issued be packed and shipped from the city without delay; that we be notified within twelve hours of the acceptance of this demand. If it is agreed to within twelve hours, we counsel forbearance on the part of all white men. If the demand is refused, or if no answer given within the time mentioned, the editor Manly, will be expelled by force.

8. It is the sense of this meeting that Mayor SP Wright and Chief of Police J.R. Melton, having demonstrated their utter incapacity to give the city a decent government and deep order therein, their continuance in office being a constant menace to the peace of this community ought forthwith to resign.

(Published in the Raleigh News and Observer, November 10, 1898.)

As one reads the *"White Declaration of Independence"* written by Christian white men in Wilmington, North Carolina, you must be impressed by the depth and sincerity of their beliefs. It all becomes clear in the first paragraph of their Declaration of White Independence:

"Believing that the Constitution of the United States contemplated a government to be carried on by an enlightened people: believing that its framers did not anticipate the enfranchisement of an ignorant population of African origin, and believing that the men of the State of North Carolina who joined in forming the Union did not contemplate for their descendants a subjection to an inferior race;"

The white American men of Wilmington North Carolina were asserting a truth—a fundamental assumption and belief—that always has and still to this very day forms the basic belief system of white Americans – either actively or passively.

These white men were not unique; they were representative of the fundamental lie/belief on which the United States of America was created namely, *"that all men are created equal ...."*

The *Declaration* continues:

> *"We, the undersigned citizens of the city of Wilmington and county of New Hanover, do hereby declare that we will no longer be ruled, and will never again be ruled, and will never again be ruled, by men of African origin. This condition we have in part endured because we felt that the consequences of the war of succession were such to deprive us of the fair consideration of many of our countrymen."*

Letters and pleas to address the wrongs and injustices perpetrated by the white men of Wilmington North Carolina in 1898 were sent to US President William McKinley by fearful black Americans and fairminded white Christian Americans. These letters and pleas fell on deaf ears. These cries for justice were not answered or addressed by the United States President, the United States Congress, the United States Courts, or any other individual or entity of power.

In 1898, the United States President, courts, and government sat idly by as the rights and lives of black Americans were totally violated, disrespected, and trampled upon by white Christian men who gave black Americans no respect.

What a Christian Minister had to say about 1898

In the aftermath of the 1898 Coup, a white minister, Rev. C.T Blackwell, pastor of First Baptist church in Wilmington North Carolina made the following excerpted comments:

"Here, the ruling motive is the outraged dignity of a proud dominant race calmly determined to assert its innate right to rule, to protect its person and property in the midst of an inferior and misguided race was secondary..."

That a few Negroes, as black Americans were called at that time, were shot was a mere incident. According to Rev. Blackwell, ***"You can't make an omelet without breaking a few eggs".*** The primary purpose was not to kill but to *educate*... In all this there is not the slightest disposition to humiliate the negroes in the high. The white people hold the Negroes in the highest respect, **so long as they observe their place and position....**"

"What is your idea as to the future good?, the good Minister was asked by a news reporter.

"There will be a lasting and wholesome mental respect between the races based on a right understanding. A change of manners on the streets for the better is already observable. It will leave a lasting good on the minds of the Negro children.... They had never seen in all their lives any strong hand, holding a rod of chastisement that they had the least fear of, or respect for, until Thursday and Friday they looked upon the rapid fires guns and Winchesters in the hands of deter-

mined masterful white men, whom they have met every day on the streets and whom they will meet in the future to respect. It struck terror in their hearts. It put new thoughts into their wooly heads. It took out of their minds a quantity of that false teaching they have received from the Record and other sources, and from the few white men who have used their parents to secure office. These children have seen, and in a sense felt the rod, which when spared too long, is as apt to spoil a childish race, as an individual child of any race of family?"

Many white Americans in power have always wanted to return to the old days of slavery, where black Americans were a second-class powerless race, relegated to serve and obey white people.

As the good minister implied, in **America it is always about maintaining the white mans' domination over all black people.**

The coup of 1898 in Wilmington North Carolina was the opening gambit of a racist game that would again put black Americans under the rule and complete domination of white Americans.

Each time black Americans made significant progress toward realizing the American dream for themselves, certain white Americans did all in their power to undermine and destroy that progress and kill their dreams.

Black Wall Street

In 1921 white men destroyed a thriving black American community in Tulsa Oklahoma known as Black Wall Street.

At the turn of the century, African (black) Americans in Tulsa, Oklahoma built the most successful Black Community and Business District in the history of the United States.... Black Wall Street. At this particular time in history, racial hatred, lynchings, Jim Crow Laws, segregation and discrimination were at an all time high. A unique community of ambitious and fearless blacks built a thriving business district in a 36-square block section of North Tulsa Oklahoma.

This small town was originally called **"Greenwood"** and **"Little Africa,"** but soon earned the nickname, **Black Wall Street** by the New York Financial District.

The community was comprised of successful black doctors, lawyers, scientists, schoolteachers, oilmen, business owners and entrepreneurs. There were hotels, churches, a hospital, schools, a bus line, private cab companies, general stores, feed and grain stores, a bowling alley, real estate offices, hair solons, restaurants, nights clubs, two movie theaters (one a 700-seater), over six hundred booming business.

There were at least ten black millionaires in Black Wall Street. **Six had private airplanes in 1921.** Recent research indicates a Paper trail where blacks were financing businesses on New York's Wall Street

Several successful entrepreneurs in Black Wall Street were in the oil business with Third World Countries during this time. The black dollar recycled and circulated throughout the black community. Many white businessmen from South Tulsa would come over to Black Wall Street to borrow money from wealthy blacks. *At that time, black Americans could not deposit their money in white banks.* Essentially they were cash rich, but power poor.

On May 31, 1921 the worst Race War in United States history erupted in the streets of Tulsa

Oklahoma. After hours of bloody fighting, Black Wall Street was bombed from the air and burned to the ground. All black Americans were rounded up and taken to Internment (concentration-type) Camps. Possibly, thousands of black men, women, and children were slaughtered. Dead bodies were dumped in the Arkansas River. Others were buried in mass graves around Tulsa. The actual death count is unknown, and to this day, remains a mystery.

(Why is the number of black Americans killed by white Christian Americans always a mystery?)

Military aircraft used to kill black Americans

The bombing of Black Wall street was the first time in American history, during non-military times that a people and their community were bombed from the air! Recent 1999 research has revealed that military aircraft were used in the bombing of homes and businesses of the black citizens of Tulsa. The facts are astoundingly clear that the Klu Klux Klan (KKK) had overwhelming support from the police, government officials, wealth businessmen and thousands of white supporters throughout Oklahoma.

The bombing and destruction of Black Wall Street was by no means an accident. It did not happen suddenly by an outburst of anger. It did not happen by two opposite races deciding to go to war. It was a well-calculated, meticulous plan to stop a major black economic development and monument that would have emulated itself across the country. The 1921 Tulsa Race Riot was part of a heinous master plan to undermine, halt, and destroy the economic success of industrious black Americans.

The so-called 1921 Tulsa Race Riot was a part of that same sinister master plan alluded to 23 years

earlier by Rev. Blackwell in Wilmington North Carolina: *"The primary purpose was not to kill but to educate."... The white people hold the Negroes in the
highest respect,* **so long as they observe their place
and position".**

The local press, authorities, the KKK and powerful white men in Oklahoma at that time set out to ig-
nite an all-out race war between whites and blacks.
They accomplished their goal.

A Dream Deferred
By Langston Hughes

What happens to a dream deferred?
Does it dry up
like a raisin in the sun?
Or fester like a sore
And then run?

Does it stink like rotten meat?
Or crust and sugar over
like a syrupy sweet?
Maybe it just sags
like a heavy load
Or does it explode?

A Special Place in Hell
By H. J. Harris

There must be a special place in hell
for those who crush hopes and dreams of other people

For those who excel and succeed
in the matters of this world
by suppressing others with hollow promises
and dreams deferred

Who discriminate by day,
and copulate by night,
with their captive prey

Who are quick to deny others
those inalienable God given rights
that they themselves so cherish.

Chapter V

In the Beginning

The Declaration of Independence

In Congress, on July 4, 1776, there was a unanimous Declaration of the thirteen United States of America that provided as follows:

"When in the Course of human events it becomes necessary for one people to dissolve the political bands which have connected them with another, and to assume among the powers of the earth, the separate and equal station to which the Laws of Nature and of Nature's God entitle them, a decent respect to the opinions of mankind requires that they should declare the causes which im-

pel them to the separation.

"We hold these truths to be self-evident, that all men are created equal, that they are endowed by their Creator with certain unalienable Rights, that among these are Life, Liberty and the pursuit of Happiness."

After enumerating the grievances against the King of Great Britain, the founding fathers, appealing to God Almighty, Supreme Judge of the world, concluded this *Declaration*:

"We, therefore, the Representatives of the United States of America, in General Congress, Assembled, appealing to the Supreme Judge of the world for the rectitude of our intentions, do, in the Name, and by Authority of the good People of the Colonies solemnly publish and declare, That these United Colonies are, and of Right ought to be Free and Independent States...

--And for the support of this Declaration, with a firm reliance on the protection of Divine Providence, we mutually pledge to each other our Lives, our Fortunes and our sacred Honor."

Sighed by John Hancock and subscribed and signed by 55 men representing the 13 Colonies.

As such powerful words were debated and written, I would imagine that these Honorable Men prayed to their God in the beginning, throughout the proceedings, and surely at the end as such lofty words were reviewed and endorsed.

Many of these men who signed this *Declaration of Independence* declaring before God that *"all men are created equal, that they are endowed by their Creator with certain unalienable Rights ... Life, Liberty, and the pursuit of Happiness ..."* were in fact being duplicitous and ingenuous because THEY OWNED SLAVES.

When Thomas Jefferson, a slave owner himself, was commissioned to draft the *Declaration of Independence*, he included a passage or clause that condemned slavery and attacked King George III's indulgence and support of the slave trade.

Jefferson wrote:

> *"He has waged cruel war against human nature itself, violating its most sacred rights of life and liberty in the persons of a distant people who never offended him, captivating and carrying them into slavery in another hemisphere, or to incur miserable death in their transportation thither.... the Christian king of Great Britain ...Determined to keep open a market where men should be bought and sold..."*

Representatives of states of South Carolina, Georgia, and other Southern states that profited directly from slavery, and Northern delegates whose ports housed and profited from slave ships caused this anti-slavery clause so passionately written by Jefferson to be completely omitted from the final version of the Declaration of Independence.

The founding fathers knew that the slavery issue was both a divisive and defining issue for the new America declaring its independence from Great Britain. John Adams, 2nd President of the United States understood the racist reality existing and totally defining the birth of this nation.

John Adams wrote in a letter to Timothy Pickering about the writing of the Declaration of Independence that Jefferson had met with him to review his original draft:

> *"A meeting we accordingly had, and conned the paper over. I was delighted with its high tone and the flights of oratory with which it abounded, especially that concerning Negro slavery, which, though I knew his Southern brethren would never suffer to pass in Congress, I certainly never would oppose."*

The omission of this anti-slavery clause, and the evidence that the slavery issue was a deal-breaker, leads one to believe that the framers of the *Declaration of Independence* never intended for black Americans to participate in the benefits of freedom and equality in America. This belief is reaffirmed in the statements made in the *White Declaration of Independence* written by the white Christian businessmen in the *Coup of 1898*.

The Original Deception

This was the original deception on which the United States was created. It is clear that a number of the founding fathers, signers of the *Declaration of Independence* and of the *United States Constitution,* were either actively or passively supportive of slavery. Many of them owned slaves. Some of these founding fathers presumably enjoyed the pleasures sinfully taken from the bodies of captive female slaves on threats of whippings or death.

In fact, it is generally accepted that Thomas Jefferson, 2nd President of the United States, writer of many of the words that would become the *Declaration of Independence*, had 5 or 6 children with Sally Hemmings, one of his favorite female slaves.

The other founding fathers supported slavery by silent acquiescence as typified by the above words of John Adams.

When we look at the historical facts out of which the United States was created, the inescapable conclusion is that America has always been willing—either actively as with the slave holding states, or passively as with the other states that benefited from slavery—to betray its religion, its moral fiber, and its sense of right and wrong when it comes to dealing fairly with black Americans.

<u>We see that the United States of America did not have a moral compass when it came to dealing with black Americans.</u>

Chapter VI

The Hundredth Monkey

As I reflected on the horrific treatment of black Americans by white Americans over the last 400 years in America, I looked for a way to understand the thinking and behaviors that have resulted from this treatment. The **Hundredth Monkey Phenomenon** provided a perfect framework for understanding what has happened to black and white Americans over the last 400 years.

The *Hundredth Monkey Phenomenon* provides that whenever a certain number of a particular species have a specific thought or demonstrate a particular behavior, then all members of that species will be aware of that thought or demonstrate that behavior.

The Hundredth Monkey
By Ken Keyes, Jr.

"The Japanese monkey, Macaca fuscata, had been observed in the wild for a period of over 30 years.

In 1952, on the island of Koshima, scientists were providing monkeys with sweet potatoes dropped in the sand. The monkeys liked the taste of the raw sweet potatoes, but they found the dirt unpleasant.

An 18-month-old female named Imo found she could solve the problem by washing the potatoes in a nearby stream. She taught this trick to her mother. Her playmates also learned this new way and they taught their mothers too.

This cultural innovation was gradually picked up by various monkeys before the eyes of the scientists.

Between 1952 and 1958 all the young monkeys learned to wash the sandy sweet potatoes to make them more palatable.

Only the adults who imitated their children learned this social improvement. Other adults kept eating the dirty sweet potatoes.

Then something startling took place. In the autumn of 1958, a certain number of Koshima monkeys were washing sweet potatoes -- the exact number is not known.

Let us suppose that when the sun rose one morning there were 99 monkeys on Koshima Island who had learned to wash their sweet potatoes.

Let's further suppose that later that morning, the hundredth monkey learned to wash potatoes.

THEN IT HAPPENED!

By that evening almost everyone in the tribe was washing sweet potatoes before eating them.

The added energy of this hundredth monkey somehow created an ideological breakthrough!

But notice.

A most surprising thing observed by these scientists was that the habit of washing sweet potatoes then jumped over the sea --

Colonies of monkeys on other islands and the mainland troop of monkeys at Takasakiyama began washing their sweet potatoes."

(From the book *"The Hundredth Monkey"* by Ken Keyes, Jr)

Thus, when a certain critical number of a particular species achieves an awareness, this new awareness may be communicated among others of that species from mind to mind.

Although the exact number may vary, this *Hundredth Monkey Phenomenon* means that when only a limited number of people know of a new way, it may remain the conscious property of these people. But, there is a point at which if only one more person tunes-in to this new awareness, a field is strengthened so that this awareness is picked up by almost everyone!

The implication of the *Hundredth Monkey Phenomenon* is that learning, and its manifested behaviors, can be transmitted from one member of a species to another member of that species without any direct communication or contact.

Could it be that this same *"Hundredth Monkey Phenomenon"* might apply to human beings, and in particular to American slaves. Are there other documented studies supporting this *"Hundredth Monkey"* learning and behavior modification phenomenon?

Behavior Modification Experiments

The most well-known experiment on the concept of inherited learning was that of Dr. William McDougall, a biologist at Harvard University.

McDougall began an experiment in 1920 to see if animals—white rats—could inherit learning. His procedure was to teach the rats a simple behavior, record how fast they learned the particular behavior, breed another generation, teach them the same behavior, and see how the rate of learning of subsequent generations compared with that of prior generations.

McDougall continued his experiment for a period of thirty years through 34 generations of mice.

McDougal would place the mice in a water maze, a pitch black tank of cold water from which there were two avenues of escape.

One escape route was well lit and easy to find, but gave the mice a painful electric shock when they tried to use it.

The other escape route was dimly lit and harder to find, but gave no electric shock and provided safe passage.

Over a period of 34 generations, McDougal found that each generation of mice learned the particular behavior – escaping from the tank without pain – faster than the prior generation.

The first generation of mice that McDougal tested took over 165 attempts before they could escape the tank avoiding the painful electric shock. By the thirty-fourth generation, the mice could find the painless escape route in about 20 attempts.

Other scientist attempted to prove or disprove McDougall's findings that behaviors could be inherited and transferred from generation to generation.

Inspired by McDougall's findings, W. E. Agar of the University of Melbourne conducted a similar experiment with mice over a period of 20 years ending in 1954. Using the same general breed of mice, Agar found the same pattern of results – hereditary learning - as McDougal.

However, Agar went a step further than McDougall in that he maintained another control group of mice that were never exposed to the water maze experiment nor trained in any way in the particular behavior maintained by the test group of mice.

There were two rather startling results of Agar's experiment:

First, when the mice in the control group that had no training in the particular behavior pattern were tested, they too learned faster with each new generation. When the mice from the control group were tested in the water maze, they were able to make a painless escape at virtually the same rate as the group of mice that had been tested and trained.

Second, the learning rate of the first generation of mice that Agar used to train in his experiment was the same as the learning rate of the last generation of mice that Dr. McDougall had trained.

In other words, the learned behavior acquired by McDougall's mice at Harvard in Cambridge Massachusetts seems to have been transferred to the same species of mice used by Agar thousands of miles away in Australia.

When F.A.E. Crew attempted to duplicate

McDougall's experiment in Edinburgh, UK, he also found that the learning rate for the mice at the start of his experiment was virtually the same as the learning rate of the last generation of McDougall's mice. Crew's first generation of test mice could escape painlessly from the water tank in only 25 attempts.

Slavery—An Experiment in Behavior Modification

What if we look at this *Hundredth Monkey Phenomenon* and apply it to the training, conditioning and treatment of the slaves—black Americans in America—particularly during the 300 years or so up to the end of the Civil War in 1865.

During this period of absolute slavery in which Africans were kidnapped from their homeland and enslaved by Christian white people, there was a systematic program of behavior modification designed to transform a black human being into an inhuman parcel of property—a black American slave.

The training of a slave is very similar to the training of the mice in the experiments of McDougall, Crew, and Agar. Slaves were basically put into a water maze—a controlled environment—America. Slaves were trained to develop and demonstrate behaviors that were pleasing to their masters. The education process was basically the same for mice and slaves: certain behaviors resulted in pain and even death, while other behaviors, those desired by the master, did not.

The difference between mice and men—the American slaves— in these comparable experiments is that men are infinitely more complex. The impact of the Slavery Experience must be examined on other levels than simple behavior patterns.

The behavior modification experiments of

McDougall, Crew, and Agar dealt with physical behavior patterns.

Let us consider the emotional and psychological patterns of thought, behavior, psyche, and outlook on life impacted by the *Slave Making Process.*

We should find that the emotional and psychological aspects of being enslaved are transferred from generation to generation—within the enslaved species as a whole—regardless of whether the particular black American was personally subjected to the *Slave Making Process.*

Chapter VII

The Making of a Slave

It is well documented that white men had developed training process that utilized physical and psychological punishment, torture, threats and intimidation to destroy the humanity of the these Kidnapped Africans. This sadistic behavior modification experience was designed to transform the Kidnapped Africans into that which was pleasing and beneficial to the white Christian masters – the black American SLAVE.

The training process of creating a slave is the same process by which rats were trained in the aforementioned laboratory experiments. The only difference is that the behavior modification process of creating a slave was not an experiment – it was an experience – a very real experience – conducted and perpetrated over 300 years.

Since the life span of a slave, due to the harsh conditions of life inflicted upon them by their masters, was undoubtedly short, 30 years is reasonable as a generation. Thus black Americans endured the direct slave experience for at least 10 generations.

Applying the Hundredth Monkey Phenomenon
to the slave making experience

Stage 1: The Capture

Let us assume that in the 1600's when the first kidnapped Africans were brought to America. The slave education had already begun. From the moment they were captured, the kidnapped Africans were intimidated, threatened, beaten and even killed to motivate them to change their behavior from whatever it was to that of a slave. They were placed in chains, strung together, and marched across the body of Africa to the sea and waiting slave ships.

The behaviors sought by the slave hunter were total submission, hopelessness, and helplessness. The goal of the slave hunter was to break the spirit of these kidnapped Africans and condition them for the greatest *"Behavior Modification"* experience the world has ever known.

Stage 2: The Cage

Europeans engaged in the slave trade built great slave castles such as Elmina Castle built in 1482 by the Portuguese on the coast of what is now Ghana. The purpose of these castles was to control the territory and serve as great holding pens for the kidnapped Africans awaiting ships to transport them to the Americas. The opening scenes in Haile Gerima's film *Sankofa* gives a vivid picture of the slave dungeons and treatment experienced by these kidnapped Africans.

In these castles and fortresses by the sea, the kidnapped Africans were herded into cages and branded like cattle with white hot branding irons that burned their flesh and made it bubble, burn and smell in that distinctive odor of death. African women were raped and abused in every way that thieves, murderers and convicts could conceive. This was the second level of the kidnapped African's conditioning and behavior modification toward becoming a slave in America.

Stage 3: The Ship

After being held in the dungeons, cells, and cages of the great slave castles, the kidnapped Africans were herded onto ships bound for America. On the slave ships, the humanity of the kidnapped Africans was further degraded by being stuffed naked into the cargo holes, shackled with chains on their wrists and their ankles, bound one to another, in spaces so tight that they could do nothing but lie in their own waste.

Stage 4: Mount Misery

Once the kidnapped Africans arrived in America, they were given over to slave trainers to receive their final educations, conditioning, training, and behavior modification. It was at the Mount Miseries of America that the slave learned to submit or die.

Here the slave learned to be totally reliant on the master.

Here the slave learned he could not think, read, or write.

Here the slave learned to fear the master and totally submit.

Reasoning analogously with the *Hundredth Monkey Phenomenon*, there would come a time when, after a finite number of kidnapped Africans had learned the behavior of a slave, at some point, all kidnapped Africans who then became the slaves of America would demonstrate the same slave behaviors, thoughts, and habits.

Stage 5: Perpetuating Slavery

Just as with the experiment where rats were taught a particular behavior, black Americans through the slavery process were taught and learned the behaviors and mindset of a slave.

This slave mindset and behavior patterns affected and inflicted not only the Kidnapped Africans who experienced the brutality of the slave making process, but also affected and inflicted virtually every black American in the United States.

Creating a slave behavior and a slave mentality in black Americans was the primary objective of the white Americans who created, and to this day control this country.

We are reminded of the words of Rev. C.T. Blackwell, the Christian minister of First Baptist Church in Wilmington, North Carolina after the violence and brutality of the *"Coup of 1898"*:

"There will be a lasting and wholesome mental respect between the races based on a right understanding. A change of manners on the streets for the better is already observable. It will leave a lasting good on the minds of the Negro children....They had never seen in all their lives any strong hand, holding a rod of chastisement that they had the least fear of, or respect for, until Thursday and Friday they looked upon the rapid fires guns and Winchesters in the hands of determined masterful white men, whom they have met every day on the streets and whom they will meet in the future to respect.

It struck terror in their hearts. It put new thoughts into their wooly heads. It took out of their minds a quantity of that false teaching they have received from the Record and other sources, and from the few white men who have used their parents to secure office. These children have seen, and in a sense felt the rod, which when spared too long, is as apt to spoil a childish race, as an individual child of any race of family."

Rev. Blackwell was affirming that the goal of white Americans through the carefully planned, consciously inflicted use of force, fear, and intimidation was to create a certain mindset and behaviors that were pleasing and acceptable to white America.

That mindset and behavior created by white America was the mindset and behavior of a slave.

Based on the application of the *Hundred Monkey Phenomenon*, virtually all black Americans have, to some degree, a slave mindset and congruent slave behaviors.

The creation of a slave by white Americans was as carefully and purposely designed and meticulously implemented as any behavior modification experiment ever conducted.

A detailed treatment of the *"slave making"* process was outlined in the famous speech of Willie Lynch delivered to Virginia slave owners in 1712.

According to an essay appearing in *"Brother Man- The Odyssey of Black Men in America- An Anthology"* Willie Lynch was a British slave owner from the West Indies who came to the United States to tell American slave owners how to keep their slaves under control. The term "lynching" is alleged to be derived from Willie Lynch's name.

Minister Louis Farrakhan quoted from Willie Lynch's speech at the Million Man March where it stunned the audience because of the cold-blooded way it described how the minds of African-Americans could be enslaved.

The Speech of Willie Lynch

"Gentlemen, I greet you here on the bank of the James River in the year of our Lord one thousand seven hundred and twelve. First, I shall thank you, the gentlemen of the Colony of Virginia, for bringing me here.

I am here to help you solve some of your problems with slaves. Your invitation reached me on my modest plantation in the West Indies where I have experimented with some of the newest and still the oldest methods of control of slaves. Ancient Rome would envy us if my program were implemented. As our boat sailed south on the James River, named for our illustrious King, whose version of the Bible we cherish. I saw enough to know that your problem is not unique. While Rome used cords of woods as crosses for standing human bodies along its highways in great numbers you are here using the tree and the rope on occasion.

I caught the whiff of a dead slave hanging from a tree a couple of miles back. You are not only losing a valuable stock by hangings, you are having uprisings, slaves are running away, your crops are sometimes left in the fields too long for maximum profit, you suffer occasional fires, your animals are killed.

Gentlemen, you know what your prob-

lems are: I do not need to elaborate. I am not here to enumerate your problems, I am here to introduce you to a method of solving them. <u>In my bag here</u>, I have a foolproof method for controlling your Black slaves. <u>I guarantee every one of you that if installed correctly it will control the slaves for at least 300 hundred years.</u> My method is simple. Any member of your family or your overseer can use it.

I have outlined a number of differences among the slaves: and I take these differences and make them bigger. I use fear, distrust, and envy for control purposes. These methods have worked on my modest plantation in the West Indies and it will work throughout the South.

Take this simple little list of differences, and think about them. On top of my list is "Age", but it is there only because it starts with an "A": the second is "Color" or shade, there is intelligence, size, sex, size of plantations, status on plantation, attitude of owners, whether the slave live in the valley, on hill, East, West, North, South, have fine hair, coarse hair, or is tall or short.

Now that you have a list of differences. I shall give you an outline of action-but before that I shall assure you that distrust is stronger than trust and envy is stronger than adulation, respect, or admiration.

The Black slave after receiving this indoctrination shall carry on and will become self re-fueling and self-generating for hundreds of years, maybe thousands. Don't forget you must pitch the old Black male vs. the young Black male, and the young Black male

against the old Black male. You must use the
dark skin slaves vs. the light skin slaves and
the light skin slaves vs. the dark skin slaves.
You must use the female vs. the male, and the
male vs. the female.

You must also have your white ser-
vants and overseers distrust all Blacks, but it
is necessary that your slaves trust and depend
on us. They must love, respect and trust only
us. Gentlemen, these kits are your keys to con-
trol. Use them. Have your wives and children
use them, never miss an opportunity. If used
intensely for one year, the slaves themselves
will remain perpetually distrustful.

Thank you, gentlemen.

As you review Willie Lynch's speech, one must wonder **what was it that he had in his bag – what was this** *"fool proof method for controlling your Black slaves?"*

Frederick Douglas, (1818 to 1895) a former slave who became an author, orator, and one of the foremost leaders in the abolitionist movement to end slavery in America spoke on and referred to the fool proof method of making a slave.

(The following information, Frederick Douglas' speech and *"Let us make a slave. What do we Need?* attributed to Willie Lynch was taken from the African-American History Resource in the AFRO-AMERICAN ALMANAC)

Frederick Douglas Speaks on Willie Lynch

"The following treatise, to the knowledgeable, will be the missing link that has been sought to explain how we were put into the condition that we find ourselves in today. It confirms the fact that the slaveholder tried to leave nothing to chance when it came to his property; his slaves. It demonstrates, how out of necessity, the slave holder had to derive a system for perpetuating his cash crop, the slave, while at the same time insulating himself from retribution by his unique property.

A careful analysis of the following handbook will hopefully change the ignorant among our people who say, "Why study slavery?" Those narrow minded people will be shown that the condition of our people is due to a scientific and psychological blue print for the perpetuation of the mental condition that allowed slavery to flourish. The slaveholder was keenly aware of the breeding principles of his livestock and the following treatise demonstrated that he thoroughly used those principles on his human live stock as well, the African Slave, and added a debilitating psychological component as well."

Let us make a slave. What do we Need?
By Willie Lynch

"First of all we need a black nigger man, a pregnant nigger woman and her baby nigger boy.

Second, we will use the same basic principle that we use in breaking a horse, combined with some more sustaining factors. **We reduce them from their natural state in nature; whereas nature provides them with the natural capacity to take care of their needs and the needs of their offspring, we break that natural string of independence from them and thereby create a dependency state so that we may be able to get from them useful production for our business and pleasure.**

CARDINAL PRINCIPLE FOR MAKING A NEGRO

For fear that our future generations may not understand the principle of breaking both horses and men, we lay down the art. For, if we are to sustain our basic economy we must break both of the beasts together, the nigger and the horse.

We understand that short range planning in economics results in periodic economic chaos, so that, to avoid turmoil in the economy, it requires us to have breadth and depth in long range comprehensive planning, articulating both skill and sharp perception. We lay down the following principles for long range comprehensive economic planning:

1) Both horse and niggers are no good to the economy in the wild or natural state.

2) Both must be broken and tied together for orderly production.

3) For orderly futures, special and particular attention must be paid to the

female and the youngest offspring.

4) Both must be crossbred to produce a variety and division of labor.

5) Both must be taught to respond to a peculiar new language.

6) Psychological and physical instruction of containment must be created for both.

We hold the above six cardinals as truths to be self-evident, based upon following discourse concerning the economics of breaking and tying the horse and nigger together...all inclusive of the six principles laid down above.

NOTE: Neither principles alone will suffice for good economics. All principles must be employed for the orderly good of the nation.

Accordingly, both a wild horse and a wild or natural nigger is dangerous even if captured, for they will have the tendency to seek their customary freedom, and, in doing so, might kill you in your sleep. You cannot rest. They sleep while you are awake and are awake while you are asleep. They are dangerous near the family house and it requires too much labor to watch them away from the house. Above all you cannot get them to work in this natural state.

Hence, both the horse and the nigger must be broken, that is break them from one form of mental life to another, keep the body and take the mind. In other words, break the will to resist.

Now the breaking process is the same for the horse and the nigger, only slightly varying in degrees. But as we said before, you must **keep your eye focused on the female and the offspring** of the horse and the nigger.

A brief discourse in offspring development will shed light on the key to sound economic principle. **Pay little attention to the generation of original breaking but concentrate on future generations.**

Therefore, if you break the female, she will break the offspring in its early years of development and, when the offspring is old enough to work, she will deliver it up to you. For her normal female protective tendencies will have been lost in the original breaking process.

For example, take the case of the wild stud horse, a female horse and an already infant horse and compare the breaking process with two captured nigger males in their natural state, a pregnant nigger woman with her infant offspring. Take the stud horse, break him for limited containment.

Completely break the female horse until she becomes very gentle whereas you or anybody can ride her in comfort. Breed the mare until you have the desired offspring. Then you can turn the stud to freedom until you need him again.

Train the female horse whereby she will eat out of your hand, and she will train the infant horse to eat of your

hand also.

When it comes to breaking the un-civilized nigger, use the same process, but vary the degree and step up the pressure so as to **do a complete reversal of the mind.**

Take the meanest and most restless nigger, strip him of his clothes in front of the remaining niggers, the female, and the nigger infant, tar and feather him, tie each leg to a different horse faced in opposite directions, set him a fire and beat both horses to pull him apart in front of the remaining niggers.

The next step is to take a bullwhip and beat the remaining nigger male to the point of death in front of the female and the infant. Don't kill him. **But put the fear of God in him, for he can be useful for future breeding.**

THE BREAKING PROCESS OF THE AFRICAN WOMAN

Take the female and run a series of tests on her to see if she will submit to you(r) desires willingly. Test her in every way, because she is the most important factor for good economic.

If she shows any signs of resistance in submitting completely to your will, do not hesitate to use the bullwhip on her to extract that last bit of bitch out of her.

Take care not to kill her, for in doing so, you spoil good economics. **When** in complete submission, she will train her offspring in the early years to submit to labor when they become of age. Understanding is the best thing.

Therefore, we shall go deeper into this area of the subject matter concerning what we have produced here in this breaking of the female nigger.

We have reversed the relationship. In her natural uncivilized state she would have a strong dependency on the uncivilized nigger male, and she would have a limited protective dependency toward her independent male offspring and would raise female offspring to be dependent like her. Nature had provided for this type of balance.

We reversed nature by burning and pulling one civilized nigger apart and bull whipping the other to the point of death--all in her presence.

By her being left alone, unprotected, with male image destroyed, the ordeal cased her to move from her psychological dependent state to a frozen independent state. In this frozen psychological state of independence she will raise her male and female offspring in reversed roles. For fear of the young male's life she will psychologically train him to be mentally weak and dependent but physically strong.

Because she has become psychologically independent, she will train her female offspring to be psychological independent as well. What have *you got? You've got the nigger woman out front and the nigger man behind and scared.* This is perfect situation for sound sleep and economics. Before the breaking process, we had to be alert and on guard at all times. Now we can sleep soundly, for out of frozen fear, his woman stand guard for us. He cannot get past her early infant slave molding process. He is a good tool, now ready to be tied to the horse at a tender age. By the time a nigger boy reaches the age of sixteen, he is soundly broken in and ready for a long life of sound and efficient work and the reproduction of a unit of good labor force.

Continually, through the breaking of uncivilized savage niggers, by throwing the nigger female savage into a frozen psychological state of independency, **by killing the protective male image, and by creating a submissive dependent mind of the nigger male slave, we have created an orbiting cycle that turns on its own axis forever, unless a phenomenon occurs and reshifts the positions of the male and female savages.**

The Breeding Process

We show what we mean by example. We breed two nigger males with two nigger females. Then we take the nigger males away from them and keep them moving and working. Say the nigger female bear a nigger female and the other bears a nigger male. both nigger females, being without influence of the nigger male image, frozen with an independent psychology, will raise him to be mentally dependent and weak, but physically strong...in other words, body over mind.

We will mate and breed them and continue the cycle.

That is good, sound, and long range comprehensive planning.

WARNING: POSSIBLE INTERLOPING NEGATIVES

Earlier, we talked about the non-economic good of the horse and the nigger in their wild or natural state; we talked out the principle of breaking and tying them together for orderly production, furthermore, **we talked about paying particular attention to the female savage and her offspring for orderly future planning; then more recently we stated that, by reversing the positions of the male and female savages we had created an orbiting cycle that turns on its own axis forever, unless phenomenon occurred, and reshifted the positions of the male and female savages.**

Our experts warned us about the possibility of this phenomenon occurring, for they say that **the mind has a strong drive to correct and recorrect itself over a period of time if it can touch some substantial original historical base**; and they advised us that the **best**

way to deal with phenomenon is to shave off the brute's mental history and create a multiplicity of phenomenon or illusions so that each illusion will twirl in its own orbit, something akin to floating balls in a vacuum. This creation of a multiplicity of phenomenon or illusions entails the principles of crossbreeding the nigger and the horse as we stated above, the purpose of which is to create a diversified division of labor.

The result of which is severance of the points of original beginnings for each spherical illusion. Since we fell (felt) that the subject matter may get more complicated as we proceed in laying down our economic plan concerning the purpose, reason, and effect of crossbreeding horses and niggers, we shall lay down the following definitional terms for future generations.

1. Orbiting cycle means a thing turning in a given pattern.

2. Axis means upon which or around which a body turns.

3. Phenomenon means something beyond ordinary conception and inspires awe and wonder.

4. Multiplicity means a great number.

5. Sphere means a globe.

6. Cross-breeding a horse means taking a horse and breeding it with an ass and you get a dumb backward ass, long-headed mule that is not reproductive nor productive by itself.

7. **Cross-breeding niggers** means taking so many drops of good white blood and putting them into as many nigger women as possible, varying the drops by the various tone that you want, and then letting them breed with each other until cycle of colors appear as you desire.

What this means is this: Put the niggers and the horse in the breeding pot, mix some asses and some good white blood and what do you get?

You got a multiplicity of colors of ass backwards, unusual niggers, running, tied to backwards ass long-headed mules, the one productive of itself, the other sterile. (The one constant, the other dying. We keep nigger constant for we may replace the mule for another tool) both mule and nigger tied to each other, neither knowing where the other came from and neither productive for itself, nor without each other.

CONTROLLED LANGUAGE

Crossbreeding completed, **for further severance from their original beginning, we must completely annihilate the mother tongue of both the nigger and the new mule and institute a new language that involves the new life's work of both**.

You know, language is a peculiar institution. It leads to the heart of people. The more a foreigner knows about the language of another country the more he is able to move through all levels of that society.

Therefore, if the foreigner is an enemy of the country, to the extent that he knows the body of the language, to that extent is the country vulnerable to attack or invasion of a foreign culture.

For example, you take the slave, **if you teach him all about your language, he will know all your secrets, and he is then no more a slave, for you can't fool him any longer and having a fool is one of the basic ingredients of and incidents to the making of the slavery system.**

The End

Many different accounts of the Slave Making Process embody the process and procedure outlined above by Willie Lynch.

As I think back on Alex Haley's TV mini series **Roots,** I remember seeing images similar in substance and essence to those described by Willie Lynch. Unruly slaves were beaten within an inch of their lives in front of the slave women and children. The white slave master had his sexual pleasures with the female slaves of his choice.

Kunta Kente tried to keep his African name and constantly ran away until the white slave master cut off his foot in front the other slaves as a barbaric lesson indelibly etched into their consciousness.

The words of Willie Lynch came to life in Hailer Grime's incredible film, *Sankofa.* Every slave making technique describe by Lynch and more were vividly portrayed in Sankofa. The words of Willie Lynch helps one understand the meaning, importance, and purpose of the chainings, torture, whippings, rapings, and disembowelment displayed by Gerima.

Sankofa gave vivid meaning to Lynch's technique of *"taking of so many drops of good white blood and putting them into as many nigger women as possible"* and *"letting them breed with each other until cycle of colors appear as you desire."*

Willie Lynch
The Hundredth Monkey
The Present Condition

Let us now consider the words of Frederick Douglas and the techniques of Willie Lynch

From the Willie Lynch writing, it was clear to Douglas that the making of a slave was based on the process by which wild animals were domesticated with added components due to the human being's mental, physical, and psychological superiority.

The process described by Willie Lynch is essentially the same process—though taken to a far higher, more complex order—that scientist used to train or modify the behavior of laboratory rats. It is the same process by which a certain monkey learns to wash his food.

In fact, the *Hundredth Monkey Phenomenon* applied to the slave making experience is scientific proof of what Douglas clearly understood – that the slave experience and mentality impacted not only those who felt the master's whip upon his back, or who experienced the unwanted intrusion of the master's lust within her body.

The slave making experience impacted not only the slave, but also the mentality, psyche, consciousness, and behavior of every black American.

What about the impact of the Slave Making Process today, in the 21st Century?

The key to the present impact lies in the *"WARNING: POSSIBLE INTERLOPING NEGATIVES"* given by Willie Lynch.

In this section Lynch recaps and summarizes the Slave Making Process saying:

> *"Earlier, we talked about the non-economic good of the horse and the nigger in their wild or natural state..."*

Translation: A black man in his natural state—in the state he was in before enslavement by the white man—has no economic good. He is of no economic value to the slave master.

What was the natural state of the Kidnapped Africans before they were transformed into American slaves?

Lynch tells us in his preamble to making a slave:

> *"First ... we need a black nigger man, a pregnant nigger woman and her baby nigger boy. ...We must reduce them from their natural state in nature: whereas nature provides them with the natural capacity to take care of their needs and the needs of their offspring,.."*

Translation: The natural state of black people was the same as the natural state of white people—nature had provided them with the natural capacity to take care of themselves and the needs of their families.

Lynch then laid out the *modus operandi* and *raison d'etre* for the slave making process:

> *"We break that natural string of independence from them and thereby create a dependency state so that we maybe able to get from them useful production for our business and pleasure."*

This further reaffirms that economics, financial benefits to certain white people, was the root cause of slavery.

Willie Lynch continues:

> *"... we talked about the principle of breaking and tying them together for orderly production"*

Translation: The principles and process of domesticating—breaking a horse (an animal) for the benefit of mankind, and of domesticating—breaking a black man were very similar. At the end of the breaking process, the horse was no longer in its natural state. It was no longer free to live, roam, procreate and do the things that horses do in the natural state. The horse, once broken, could only serve and benefit its master.

If by some stroke of fate, the broken horse, and especially its offspring, were released to the wild and returned to its natural state, it would not have the skills to survive.

The kidnapped Africans, after they had been domesticated—broken by Christian white men—became the black American slaves. At the end of this *"breaking"* process, the kidnapped African was no longer in its natural state. It was now a black American slave. This slave was no longer free to live, and move about, procreate, and do the things that black men did in their natural state. The slave, once broken, could only serve and benefit its master.

Lynch continued,

"…. we talked about paying particular attention to the female savage and her offspring for orderly future planning"

Translation: Once the female was broken, she would teach her young how to be a slave. Her offspring would have no knowledge of their natural state. They would only know how to be a slave. They would only know that which the master wanted them to know so that they could serve him.

A slave mother, heeding to her natural instincts to nurture and protect her young would only teach her children that which they need to know to survive as a slave.

According to Lynch, the purpose of the breaking process was to create *"a complete reversal of the mind"*

This was accomplished by consistently creating fear and hopelessness in the minds of the slaves. As Lynch described it:

"Take the meanest and most restless nigger, strip him of his clothes in front of the remaining niggers, the female, and the nigger infant, tar and feather him, tie each leg to a different horse faced in opposite directions, set him a fire and beat both horses to pull him

apart in front of the remaining niggers.

The next step is to take a bullwhip and beat the remaining nigger male to the point of death in front of the female and the infant. Don't kill him. But put the fear of God in him, for he can be useful for future breeding. "

The purpose of the planned brutality was to change the behavior of the kidnapped Africans to the behavior of a slave. **This process of Slave Making, perpetrated by white Christian Americans upon their captive prey, was the ultimate experiment in behavior modification.**

These slave thoughts, emotions, behaviors and outlook on life, created and reinforced by the slave master, became imbedded deep within the psyche of the black American slaves.

The role reversal between male and female slaves, based on these thoughts, emotions, behaviors, and outlook on life becomes the foundation on which the relationship between black American men and women is based.

In the words of Willie Lynch,

"... by reversing the positions of the male and female savages we had created an orbiting cycle that turns on its own axis forever, unless phenomenon occurred, and reshifted the positions of the male and female savages."

The Key—The Missing Link

This is the key that Frederick Douglas referred to as,

"...the missing link that has been sought to explain how we were put into the condition that we find ourselves in today."

This is the key that will explain the condition of black Americans TODAY at the beginning of the Twenty-First Century.

As Willie Lynch stated, this reversal of roles in black American men and women, and the resultant thoughts, emotions, behaviors and outlook, <u>will continue until a phenomenon occurs to reshift—change—them.</u>

The thoughts, emotions, behaviors, and outlook on life taken together represent a *Slave Consciousness*. As long as the *Slave Consciousness* created over the last 400 years by white Americans for their own benefit remains, the condition of black Americans WILL NOT CHANGE.

So now black Americans and white American must realize a profound fact: virtually nothing has been done to or on behalf of black Americans to undue the *Slave Consciousness* created by 400 years of slavery.

Neither the outlawing of the slave trade in 1807, not the Emancipation Proclamation, nor the Thirteenth Amendment to United States Constitution, nor the Civil Rights Acts of 1866 or 1964, nor the US Supreme Court decision of 1954 desegregating the public schools, nor any other legislation or program has done anything to destroy or effectively change the *Slave Consciousness* that exists in black Americans.

Further, reaffirming the *Hundredth Monkey Phenomenon*, this Slave Consciousness, to varying degrees, affects every black American, living or dead, in this country.

The Updated Doll Experiment of 2006

In 2006 a young black American filmmaker did an updated version of Dr. Kenneth and Mamie Clark's famous Doll Experiment that showed the negative impact of segregation in the education of black American children.

The results of the Updated Doll Experiment were virtually the same as Drs. Clark's results 50 years earlier. In other words, 50 years after public school desegregation, the great society initiatives, affirmative action, and a host of social programs designed to help black Americans overcome the damages caused by segregation and discrimination, NOTHING HAS-CHANGED.

Changing the Slave Consciousness

When we look at the condition of black Americans in America today, the obvious question is: *Why are we where we are? Why, over 140 years after the Emancipation Proclamation, the Thirteenth Amendment, and the end of the Civil War, aren't we further along the road to power and prosperity as a people?*

Why is it that other nationalities of people can come to this country and, in a relatively short period of time, move ahead of black Americans in power and prosperity?

The Irish came to America in the late 1800's and within less than a 100 years they have become an integral part of the American power structure. The Italians, Jews, Chinese, Koreans, Indians, Hispanics and just about any other nationality are able to come to America and be successful. In a relatively short period of time they are able to achieve power and wealth, especially in proportion to their numbers.

Presently we see the Hispanics doing the same thing – achieving power and wealth in America. In the last 50 years, Hispanics are opening more banks, starting more businesses, and generally moving past black Americans in the realm of power and wealth. For example in 2006, in the town of Wilmington, North Carolina located within New Hanover County with a population of over 170,000 citizens, there are at least 4 first class Hispanic restaurants and not a single first class black restaurant. How do you explain this difference when we consider that there are approximately 28,000 black Americans and roughly 4,000 Hispanics in New Hanover County?

Are the Hispanics more industrious? Is capital more readily available? The answer is much more complicated.

No Black Partnerships

When you consider the legal and real estate professions, one of the things that you rarely find in the operation of black businesses is true PARTNERSHIPS.

You will sometimes find black lawyers, or black accountants, or black real estate brokers, black contractors, or even black doctors sharing office space, with numerous names listed on the entrance door.

If you check further, you will usually find that one of the black professionals is the owner or leaseholder, and the others are simply subletting space. Or, you may find that these black American professionals are simply sharing space and expenses. There is no sharing of management or of revenues.

Am I saying that black businesspeople never work together in true partnerships with shared management, expenses, and revenues? No, not always, but such partnerships are rare.

When considering other races or ethnic groups, working together in some form of partnership is a key element to their collective success.

Why does it appear to be difficult for black American business people, or for black Americans in general to be able to work together in partnership?

One primary reason that black Americans may not be able to work together in partnership is that partnerships require trust—trust in yourself and trust in each other.

Let us reflect on the closing sentences of Willie Lynch's speech in 1712 on the banks of the James River with respect to his Slave Making techniques:

"You must also have your white servants and overseers distrust all Blacks, but it is necessary that your slaves trust and depend on us. They must love, respect and trust only us. Gentlemen, these kits are your keys to control. Use them. Have your wives and children use them, never miss an opportunity. If used intensely for one year, the slaves themselves will remain perpetually distrustful."

The white slave master bred fear, distrust, and total dependence into the fiber and being of the black American slaves. Fear, distrust and total dependence in thought, emotions, behavior, and world outlook was the desired end-result of the behavior modification process of making a slave.

Applying the Hundredth Monkey Phenomenon to the Slave Making Process

Applying the *Hundredth Monkey Phenomenon* to this Slave Making Process leads to the inevitable conclusion: over the 350 years of absolute slavery, the qualities of fear, distrust and total dependence was so bread into black American slaves that, after a finite number of slaves were created, there came a time when these negative qualities appeared and were imbedded in the psyche and fiber of virtually every black American —slave or free, living or dead.

This explains the *Slave Consciousness* through the end of the Civil War. **What about after the Civil War when slavery was ended and made illegal?**

Did there come a time when the freed slaves were able to shake off and eliminate the Slave Consciousness that had been inflicted upon them for so long?

Yes, there was a time after the Civil War when the freed slaves and well-intentioned white Christians worked together to change the *Paradigm of Slavery*. This period was the Reconstruction. However, while good white Americans and recently freed slaves and free black Americans worked together to change the *Paradigm of Slavery*, many white Americans in leadership positions did all they could to undermine their efforts.

After the Civil War, the white Americans in power changed their tactics but continued to perpetuate the *Paradigm of Slavery* created by the Willie Lynch slave making principles. The specifics of the Slave Making Process were changed, but the goal remained the same: domination of black Americans by white Americans.

Chapter VIII

The Civil War and Reconstruction

The Civil War

The American Civil War (1861 – 1865) was a war in the United States between the *Union* – predominantly northern states that did not support slavery of black Americans and the *Confederacy* – predominantly southern states that supported and practiced slavery.

The Civil War was a predictable end result of the contradictions imbedded in the creation of America. It was not a war started by righteous God fearing Christian Americans attacking the slavery-based Southern states to secure those God given inalienable rights of life, liberty and the pursuit of happiness for the long-suffering black American slaves.

The Civil War was started by slave-owning Southerners seeking to consolidate their robust slave-based, FREE LABOR economy so that only the South would reap the rewards of the blood, sweat, and tears of the black American slave's perpetual bondage.

The Heritage of Slavery

In American today, many white Americans seek to celebrate the Civil War as part of their heritage. Many states such as South Carolina and Georgia incorporate symbols of the Confederacy into their state flags. Organizations such as the Daughters of the Confederacy proudly honor their confederate heritage.

What is that confederate heritage with which many white Americans proudly identify? It is a heritage of slavery, injustice and total disrespect for the humanity of black Americans. The *"real"* Confederate heritage was an addiction **to FREE SLAVE LABOR** which was so strong that white Christian American southerners gave their lives to perpetuate it.

Many, who to this day honor this Confederate heritage, will tell you that the Civil War was not about slavery at all. They say that the Civil War was about a *"way of life"* or *"states rights"*, not slavery.

But then one must ask, what *"states right"* was the Confederacy fighting to protect?

What *"way of life"* or *"states right"* was so important that the Southern states of the United States would start a Civil War by bombarding Fort Sumter in South Carolina.

Was it the right to plant cotton, or own ships and businesses? Or, perhaps it was the right to live on lavish plantations, and have garden parties on hot summer afternoons.

No! The only right, *"states right"* or otherwise —the only *"way of life"*—that caused the civil war was the **RIGHT TO OWN, TRADE IN, AND RECEIVE THE BENEFITS OF SLAVES AND THE SLAVERY OF BLACK AMERICANS.**

The American Civil War was probably the most costly war ever fought in terms of American deaths and casualties. Over the four years of the Civil War, the best estimate most often quoted is that 620,000 Americans died from battle, disease, etc. The Union armies lost 360,222 men and the Confederate armies lost 258,000 men. **With such an incredible death toll, it is clear that the issue of slavery of black Americans was at the heart and core of America's vision of itself as a nation.**

The Reconstruction

The Reconstruction was a period in American History, 1863 through 1877, where the issues raised by the Civil War were to be addressed and resolved. It was during this 14 year period that the following primary issues were to be resolved:

1. Returning the southern states that had seceded from the union back into the United States.
2. The status of former Confederate leaders.
3. The integration of former slaves and free black Americans into the legal, political, economic, and social system.

The implementation of the Reconstruction, and the controversy and violence that it caused, leads one to believe that freeing the slaves was not a moral issue with most white Americans in power at that time.

In a sense, the Reconstruction essentially began with President Abraham Lincoln's *Emancipation Proclamation.*

The Emancipation Proclamation

Although The Emancipation Proclamation is often touted by black and white Americans as the document that freed the slaves, and Abraham Lincoln is called *"The Great Emancipator"*, the truth is far less noble.

First, Lincoln was a politician. We do not know his personal thoughts on the issue of slavery—whether or not he thought it was morally right or wrong. What we do know is that Lincoln was pressured by the abolitionist and radical Republicans to issue an order freeing the slaves. It was nearly two years after the Civil War started on April 12, 1861 that President Lincoln finally issued the *Emancipation Proclamation* on January 1, 1863.

The Emancipation Proclamation
did not free all slaves

Contrary to popular belief, the *Emancipation Proclamation* was very limited in many ways.

First, it applied only to states that had seceded from the Union, leaving slavery untouched in the loyal Border States.

Second, it exempted part of the Confederacy that had already come under Northern control.

Third, the promised freedom for the slaves depended upon Union military victory.

Although the *Emancipation Proclamation* did not immediately free a single slave, it transformed the character of the war. After the *Emancipation Proclamation*, the advance of Union troops in effect freed the slaves in the conquered territories and advanced the domain of freedom. **Freeing the slaves was more of a military tactic than a moral imperative.**

In addition, the Proclamation provided that black men would be accepted in the Union Army and Navy.

A careful reading of the *Emancipation Proclamation* together with Lincoln's political motives for making the Proclamation, demonstrate and confirm that political expediency and not moral fiber was its *raison d'etre*.

By freeing only those slaves in states and parts of states that were in rebellion, Lincoln left slavery in tact and in a sense condoned it in states that were not in rebellion. I am certain that consideration was given to the possibility that if the slaves knew that they would be freed when the Union Army captured their area, these slaves, wanting their freedom, would be inclined to aid and assist in defeating the Confederacy.

In addition, offering slaves a chance to serve in the Union Army or Navy, could not only undermine the Confederacy but also be a military advantage. By the end of the Civil War, almost 200,000 black soldiers and sailors fought for the Union Army.

The Emancipation Proclamation

January 1, 1863
A Transcription
By the President of the United States of America: A Proclamation.

Whereas, on the twenty-second day of September, in the year of our Lord one thousand eight hundred and sixty-two, a proclamation was issued by the President of the United States, containing, among other things, the following, to wit:

"That on the first day of January, in the year of our Lord one thousand eight hundred and sixty-three, *all persons held as slaves within any State or designated part of a State, the people whereof shall then be in rebellion against the United States, shall be then, thenceforward, and forever free;* and the Executive Government of the United States, including the military and naval authority thereof, will recognize and maintain the freedom of such persons, and will do no act or acts to repress such persons, or any of them, in any efforts they may make for their actual freedom.

"That the Executive will, on the first day of January aforesaid, by proclamation, designate the States and parts of States, if any, in which the people thereof, respectively, shall then be in rebellion against the United States; and the fact that any State, or the people thereof, shall on that day be, in good faith, represented in the Congress of the United States by members chosen thereto at elections wherein a majority of the qualified voters of such State shall have participated, shall, in the absence of strong countervailing testimony, be deemed conclusive evidence that such State, and the people thereof, are not then in rebellion against the United States."

"Now, therefore I, Abraham Lincoln, President of the United States, by virtue of the power in me vested as Commander-in-Chief, of the Army and Navy of the United States in time of actual armed rebellion against the authority and government of the United States, and as a fit and necessary war measure for suppressing said rebellion, do, on this first day of January, in the year of our Lord one thousand eight hundred and sixty-three, and in accordance with my purpose so to do publicly proclaimed for the full period of one hundred days, from the day first above mentioned, order and designate as the States and parts of States wherein the people thereof respectively, are this day in rebellion against the United States, the following, to wit:

"Arkansas, Texas, Louisiana, (except the Parishes of St. Bernard, Plaquemines, Jefferson, St. John, St. Charles, St. James Ascension, Assumption, Terrebonne, Lafourche, St. Mary, St. Martin, and Orleans, including the City of New Orleans) Mississippi, Alabama, Florida, Georgia, South Carolina, North Carolina, and Virginia, (except the forty-eight counties designated as West Virginia, and also the counties of Berkley, Accomac, Northampton, Elizabeth City, York, Princess Ann, and Norfolk, including the cities of Norfolk and Portsmouth[)], and which excepted parts, are for the present, left precisely as if this proclamation were not issued.

"And by virtue of the power, and for the purpose aforesaid, I do order and declare that all persons held as slaves within said designated States, and parts of States, are, and henceforward shall be free; and that the Executive government of the United States, including the military and naval authorities thereof, will recognize and maintain the freedom of said persons.

"And I hereby enjoin upon the people so declared to be free to abstain from all violence, unless in necessary self-defense; and I recommend to them that, in all cases when allowed, they labor faithfully for reasonable wages.

"And I further declare and make known, that such persons of suitable condition, will be received into the armed service of the United States to garrison forts, positions, stations, and other places, and to man vessels of all sorts in said service.

"And upon this act, sincerely believed to be an act of justice, warranted by the Constitution, upon military necessity, I invoke the considerate judgment of mankind, and the gracious favor of Almighty God.

"In witness whereof, I have hereunto set my hand and caused the seal of the United States to be affixed.

"Done at the City of Washington, this first day of January, in the year of our Lord one thousand eight hundred and sixty three, and of the Independence of the United States of America the eighty-seventh."

By the President: ABRAHAM LINCOLN

WILLIAM H. SEWARD,
Secretary of State.

From the issuance of the Emancipation Proclamation through the end of the Reconstruction, white Americans implemented a new type of slavery. The true freedom of black American slaves was compromised and undermined at every turn.

With Lincoln's assassination, Andrew Johnson, a Southern Democrat became president. President Johnson had his own plan for Presidential Reconstruction that called for general amnesty and restoration of property – except for slaves - to the defeated Southern Confederates who would swear loyalty to the Union.

In Special Field Order 15, General William Tecumseh Sherman set aside part of coastal South Carolina, Georgia, and Florida to be settled exclusively by black Americans. The black settlers, many of whom were former slaves were supposed to receive possessory title to 40 acres of land and a mule.

It was President Andrew Johnson who took the so-called 40 acres back from the black Americans and returned it to its former owners—white Americans, Confederates—who had fought the against the Union. Eventually Johnson aligned himself with the Southern white former confederates under the theme, *"white men alone must manage the South."*

Immediately upon taking office, President Johnson attempted his own brand of Presidential Reconstruction creating a racist atmosphere at the highest level of government. He handed out thousands of pardons to former Confederates in routine fashion and allowed the South to set up *"black codes,"* severe state laws that limited the freedom of former slaves and essentially maintained slavery under another name.

Chapter IX

The New Slavery

With President Johnson in office, the Southern states were slow to ratify the Thirteenth Amendment prohibiting slavery. These states used the *Black Codes* to re-establish white supremacy. These black codes were basically attempts to control black labor. Freed former slaves were prohibited from working except as field hands. Black Americans who refused to sign labor contracts could be punished. Unemployed black men could be seized and auctioned to planters as laborers. Black children could be taken from their families and made to work.

The new Black Codes were essentially slavery without the chain.

Typical Black Codes in South Carolina and Mississippi provided:

"Negroes must make annual contracts for their labor in writing; if they should run away from their tasks, they forfeited their wages for the year. Whenever it was required of them they must present licenses (in a town from the mayor; elsewhere from a member of the board of police of the beat) citing their places of residence and authorizing them to work. Fugitives from labor were to be arrested and carried back to their employers. Five dollars a head and mileage would be allowed such negro catchers. It was made a misdemeanor, punishable with fine or imprisonment, to persuade a freedman to leave his employer, or to feed the runaway. Minors were to be apprenticed, if males until they were twenty-one, if females until eighteen years of age. Such corporal punishment as a father would administer to a child might be inflicted upon apprentices by their masters. Vagrants were to be fined heavily, and if they could not pay the sum, they were to be hired out to service until the claim was satisfied. Negroes might not carry knives or firearms unless they were licensed so to do. It was an offense, to be punished by a fine of $50 and imprisonment for thirty days, to give or sell intoxicating liquors to a negro. When negroes could not pay the fines and costs after legal proceedings, they were to be hired at public outcry by the sheriff to the lowest bidder....

"In South Carolina persons of color contracting for service were to be known as "servants," and those with whom they contracted, as "masters." On farms the hours of labor would be from sunrise to sunset daily, except on Sunday. The negroes were to get out of bed at dawn.

Time lost would be deducted from their wages, as would be the cost of food, nursing, etc., during absence from sickness. <u>Absentees on Sunday must return to the plantation by sunset. House servants were to be at call at all hours of the day and night on all days of the week. They must be "especially civil and polite to their masters, their masters' families and guests," and they in return would receive "gentle and kind treatment."</u> Corporal and other punishment was to be administered only upon order of the district judge or other civil magistrate. A vagrant law of some severity was enacted to keep the negroes from roaming the roads and living the lives of beggars and thieves."

In spite of the fact that the Confederacy lost the Civil War, and Abraham Lincoln signed the *Emancipation Proclamation*, and the United States Constitution was modified by the Thirteenth, Fourteenth and Fifteenth Amendments, white Christian Americans, actively or passively, engaged in a systematic program to limit and restrict the freedom of former slaves.

There developed throughout the South and indeed throughout the country an atmosphere of threats, intimidation, and death to former slaves—black Americans—who were trying to experience the life, liberty, and quiet enjoyment promised nearly 100 years ago in the birth of the United States, and now reaffirmed through the 13th and 14th Amendments.

It should be noted that the white Americans in power, Democrats and Republicans, struggled over guaranteeing citizenship and civil rights to black Americans for nearly three (3) years after the end of the Civil War. Though the 13th Amendment to the United States Constitution abolishing slavery was ratified in 1865, it would take nearly three more years (July 28, 1868) and the overriding of President Andrew Johnson's veto before the 14th Amendment guaranteeing citizenship and federal civil rights to black Americans would be ratified.

Still, even with the ratification of the 13th and 14th Amendments, the white Christian Americans in power could not bring themselves to giving, guaranteeing, and protecting the right to vote of black Americans, former slaves.

White Christian Americans inflicted one brutality after another designed to *"educate"* the former slaves to the reality of their condition.

Some of the many injustices and brutalities perpetrated by white Christian Americans include:

May 1, 1866: Racial violence rages in Memphis, Tennessee for three days as white Americans attack and assault black Americans throughout the city. Forty-eight (48) people, nearly all black Americans were killed. Hundreds of black American homes, churches, and schools were destroyed and burned.

July 30, 1866: Riots break out in New Orleans, Louisiana. A mob of white Americans attack black Americans and Radical Republicans attending a black Suffrage (voting rights) convention, killing 40 people.

September 1868: Black American elected officials are ousted from the Georgia state legislature. The leading newspaper at the time, the Atlanta Constitution, justifying this ouster declaring: "The Negro is unfit to rule the State." President Grant, after appeal by the ousted black American legislators, took a year to get them readmitted.

Fall, 1869: Violence against black Americans continues throughout the south. In October, Abram

Colby, a former slave who was duly elected to the Georgia legislature, was kidnapped and whipped.

Members of the Ku Klux Klan had beaten Colby savagely in 1869 in an attempt to end his political activities as a Radical Republican, after earlier efforts to bribe the black legislator had failed. Colby, permanently injured by the assault that nearly killed him, defied intimidation to remain active in eastern Georgia politics.

In 1872 Colby was called to Washington to testify before a joint House and Senate committee investigating reports of Southern violence. Below is an excerpt of his testimony:

Colby: On the 29th of October 1869, [the Klansmen] broke my door open, took me out of bed, took me to the woods and whipped me three hours or more and left me for dead. They said to me, "Do you think you will ever vote another damned Radical ticket?" I said, "If there was an election tomorrow, I would vote the Radical ticket." They set in and whipped me a thousand licks more, with sticks and straps that had buckles on the ends of them.

Question: What is the character of those men who were engaged in whipping you?

Colby: Some are first-class men in our town. One is a lawyer, one a doctor, and some are farmers. They had their pistols and they took me in my night-clothes and carried me from home. They hit me five thousand blows. I told President Grant the same that I tell you now. They told me to take off my shirt. I said, "I never do that for any man." My drawers fell down about my feet and they took hold of them and tripped me up. Then they pulled my shirt up over my head. They said I had voted for Grant and had carried the Negroes against them. About two days before they whipped me they offered me $5,000 to go with them and said they would pay me $2,500 in cash if I would let another man go to the legislature in my place. I told them that I would not do it if they would give me all the county was worth.

The worst thing was my mother, wife and daughter were in the room when they came. My little daughter begged them not to carry me away. They drew up a gun and actually frightened her to death. She never got over it until she died. That was the part that grieves me the most.

Question: How long before you recovered from the effects of this treatment?

Colby: I have never got over it yet. They broke something inside of me. I cannot do any work now, though I always made my living before in the barbershop, hauling wood, etc.

Question: You spoke about being elected to the next legislature?

Colby: Yes, sir, but they run me off during the election. They swore they would kill me if I stayed. The Saturday night before the election I went to church.

When I got home they just peppered the house with shot(s) and bullets.
Question: Did you make a general canvas there last fall?
Colby: No, sir. I was not allowed to. No man can make a free speech in my county. I do not believe it can be done anywhere in Georgia.
Question: You say no man can do it?
Colby: I mean no Republican, either white or colored.

As you read Colby's testimony, the question arises: If white Americans would do this to a duly elected public official, what would white Americans, these *"first-class men ... a lawyer, a doctor, a farmer"*, do to ordinary former slaves, black Americans freed by the *Emancipation Proclamation* and the 13th Amendment?

One of the most vivid pictures of what it was like to be a former slave is given in an excerpt from *Senate Report 693, 46th Congress, 2nd Session (1880)*. Reprinted in Dorothy Sterling, editor, *The Trouble They Seen: The Story of Reconstruction in the Words of African Americans*. New York: Da Capo Press, 1994, Dorothy Sterling, editor.

Not Free Yet

Freed by the Emancipation Proclamation in 1865, former slave Henry Adams testified before the U.S. Senate fifteen years later about the early days of his freedom, describing white planters' unfair labor practices and the violent, intimidating atmosphere in which ex-slaves felt compelled to work for their former masters.

The white men read a paper to all of us colored people telling us that we were free and could go where we pleased and work for who we pleased. The man I belonged to told me it was best to stay with him. He said, "The bad white men was mad with the Negroes because they were free and they would kill you all for fun." He said, stay where we are living and we could get protection from our old masters.

I told him I thought that every man, when he was free, could have his rights and protect themselves. He said, "The colored people could never protect themselves among the white people. So you had all better stay with the white people who raised you and make contracts with them to work by the year for one-fifth of all you make.

And next year you can get one-third, and the next you maybe work for one-half you make. We have contracts for you all to sign, to work for one-twentieth you make from now until the crop is ended, and then next year you all can make another crop and get more of it."

I told him I would not sign anything. I said, "I might sign to be killed. I believe the white people is trying to fool us." But he said again, "Sign this contract so I can take it to the Yankees and have it recorded." All our colored people signed it but myself and a boy named Samuel Jefferson. All who lived on the place was about sixty, young and old.

On the day after all had signed the contracts, we went to cutting oats. I asked the boss, "Could we get any of the oats?" He said, "No; the oats were made before you were free." After that he told us to get timber to build a sugar-mill to make molasses. We did so.

On the 13th day of July 1865 we started to pull fodder. I asked the boss would he make a bargain to give us half of all the fodder we would pull. He said we may pull two or three stacks and then we could have all the other. I told him we wanted half, so if we only pulled two or three stacks we would get half of that. He said, "All right." We got that and part of the corn we made. We made five bales of cotton but we did not get a pound of that. We made two or three hundred gallons of molasses and only got what we could eat. We made about eight-hundred bushel of potatoes; we got a few to eat. We split rails three or four weeks and got not a cent for that.

In September I asked the boss to let me go to Shreveport. He said, "All right, when will you come back?" I told him "next week." He said, "You had better carry a pass." I said, "I will see whether I am free by going without a pass."

I met four white men about six miles south of Keachie, De Soto Parish. One of them asked me who I belonged to. I told him no one. So him and two others struck me with a stick and told me they were going to kill me and every other Negro who told them that they did not belong to anyone. One of them who knew me told the others, "Let Henry alone for he is a hard-working nigger and a good nigger." They left me and I then went on to Shreveport. I seen over twelve colored men and women, beat, shot and hung between there and Shreveport.

Sunday I went back home. The boss was not at home. I asked the madame, "where was the boss?" She says, "Now, the boss; now, the boss! You should say 'master' and 'mistress' -- and shall or leave. We will not have no nigger here on our place who cannot say 'mistress' and 'master.' You all are not free yet and will not be until Congress sits, and you shall call every white lady 'missus' and every white man 'master.'"

During the same week the madame takin' a stick and beat one of the young colored girls, who was about fifteen years of age and who is my sister, and split her back. The boss came next day and take this same girl (my sister) and whipped her nearly to death, but in the contracts he was to hit no one any more.

After the whipping a large number of young colored people taken a notion to leave. On the 18th of September I and eleven men and boys left that place and started for Shreveport. I had my horse along. My brother was riding him, and all of our things was packed on him. Out come about forty armed men (white) and shot at us and takin' my horse. Said they were going to kill ever' nigger they found leaving their masters; and taking all of our clothes and bed-clothing and money. I had to work away to get a white man to get my horse.

Then I got a wagon and went to peddling, and had to get a pass, according to the laws of the parishes, to do so. In October I was searched for pistols and robbed of $250 by a large crowd of white men and the law would do nothing about it.

The same crowd of white men broke up five churches (colored). When any of us would leave the white people, they would take everything we had, all the money that we made on their places. They killed many hundreds of my race when they were running away to get freedom.

After they told us we were free -- even then they would not let us live as man and wife together. And when we would run away to be free, the white people would not let us come on their places to see our mothers, wives, sisters, or fathers. We was made to leave or go back and live as slaves.

To my own knowledge there was over two thousand colored people killed trying to get away after the white people told us we were free in 1865. This was between Shreveport and Logansport.

It was blatantly clear America faced a true dilemma in determining how to deal with or relate to black Americans. In 1870 President Grant proposed a treaty of annexation with Santo Domingo in an attempt to find land for freed slaves to settle. Grant proposed to relocate freed slaves to an island in the Caribbean, now the Dominican Republic. The proposal never got off the ground.

The violence against black American continues

April 13, 1873: *The Colfax Massacre*. The Knights of the White Camellia, the White League, a paramilitary group intent on securing white rule in Louisiana, engaged in battle with Louisiana's almost all-black state militia. The result death toll was staggering. Two or three members of the White League were killed and estimates from 70 to 280 black Americans were killed. Many of the black Americans were killed in cold blood after they had surrendered.

The End of Reconstruction

In 1877 following a bitter disputed presidential election between Republican Rutherford B. Hayes and Democrat Samuel Tilden in which both candidates claimed victory, the stage was set to completely undermine the spirit and laws that ended slavery and gave black Americans the same rights and privileges under the United States Constitution as white Americans.

The Republicans, the party of Abraham Lincoln, the party that had championed the Reconstruction and the fair and just task of educating the freed slaves and integrating them into the American way of life, betrayed all black Americans. In behind-the-scenes, back-room deals, the Republicans agreed to remove troops from the south and effectively end the Reconstruction.

This act by the Republican Party returned the fate of black Americans in the south to the same white Americans who had enslaved them prior to the Civil War. The euphemistic term for this new arrangement was *States Rights*.

The Final Blow

The final blow to the aspirations of freedom, justice and equality for black Americans came in the form of a United States Supreme Court decision in **Plessy v. Ferguson**, 163 U.S. 536 (1896).

In this case, the United States Supreme Court ruled that segregation in public facilities was legal and that states could prohibit the use of public facilities by black Americans.

Plessy v. Ferguson and its application in a *"States Rights"* context was used as the legal foundation for the next 60 years of discrimination, abuse, intimidation, and denial of basic human rights of life, liberty, and the pursuit of happiness promised in the United States Constitution.

The Reconstruction under Plessy v. Ferguson morphed into the New American Slavery that continues in new and different forms until this very day.

Chapter X

Thank God for Television

The primary difference between civil rights struggle of black people before the 1950's and the struggle after the 1950's was the advent of television.

America's track record in dealing with black Americans shows the absence of a true *moral compass*. Stark incidents like the aftermath of Hurricane Katrina open the festering wound of unresolved racism that continuously exists beneath the outward façade displayed by the spirit that is America. This festering wound is a direct result of the *Paradigm of Slavery* that holds America solidly in its grip.

Through television, the whole world can see how America actually treats black Americans. The whole world can see in vivid pictures that there is a contradiction between the image America projects to the world—*land of the free, home of the brave, with liberty and justice for all*—and the reality of how it treats its own black Americans.

When the world sees the *Leader of the Free World* leave its black American citizens stranded without food or water for nearly a week, it questions the moral authority of the United States. How can America bring freedom, justice, and democracy to other sovereign nations when it cannot or will not give life, liberty, and the pursuit of happiness to all of its own citizens?

Since America does not like to appear a fraud or deceitful in the eyes of the world, television images of black Americans suffering result in public promises and picturesque press conferences delivering solemn commitments to make things right.

The reality is that once the glare of the news cameras of CNN and other international news organizations disappear, the plight of black Americans will fall once more to the bottom of America's priorities.

When significant, though fleeting changes take place in the way white Americans in power treat black Americans, it is not motivated by a righteous *Moral Compass*, but rather by the lens of international press cameras that expose the *Paradigm of Racism* so firmly entrenched in the fabric of America.

For many black Americans – *"My country, 'tis of thee, sweet land of liberty.."* applies mainly to white Americans. This was demonstrated in the 1950's and 1960's when the world through television saw white Americans in authority—southern policemen who were charged with protecting all citizens—spraying black American men, women, and children with fire hoses, letting trained dogs attack black citizens trying to exercise their constitutional rights.

The rest of the world saw images of James Earl Chaney, Andrew Goodman, and Michael H. Schwerner, three young civil rights workers whose bullet riddled bodies were buried in an earthen dam in the southern state of Mississippi.   Images of Viola Liuzzo—a white Christian American woman who went to Alabama to help black Americans in their struggle for civil rights – shot dead by white racist Americans shocked the world in its brutality.

Television gave the whole world a picture of the lifeless bodies of four little black American girls killed on a Sunday morning by white American racists who placed dynamite at the Sixteenth Street Baptist Church in Birmingham, Alabama.

Through television the rest of the world saw that America was living a lie. This shamed America and gave good and righteous Americans, black and white, Christian, Jews, Gentiles, and others a chance to help America live up to its creed.

Television projected the braveness of the *Greensboro Four*, four students at A & T State University in Greensboro, North Carolina, who started the civil rights sit-ins to integrate eating facilities in the south.

It was television that brought a little old white lady to join the *Greensboro Four* as they sat-in at a lunch counter harassed and spat upon by white Americans who opposed integration. Joseph McNeil, one of the *Four* said that the white lady asked him, *"Why did it take so long for black people to sit in and force integration?"*

My questions to this little old white lady would have been,

"Why did it take her so long to come forth and declare that segregation was immoral and wrong?"

"Didn't she know it was wrong before those four young men risked their lives to secure what had been promised in the Declaration of independence?"

"Why did she and other white Christian Americans stand back and say nothing for so many years?"

It is through the power of television that the world can see the contradictions and racism that still exist in 21st Century America. The images seen on television remind citizens of the world that *all is not well in America*. Many Americans delude themselves into thinking that America has lived up to its creed, and that the *Paradigm of Racism* was long ago resolved by integration and affirmative action.

But, television serves as a stark reminder of the truth that is America: whether the aftermath of Hurricane Katrina in 2005, or the vicious beating of Rodney King by Los Angeles police officers in 1991, or the dragging of James Byrd, Jr. to his death by white American racists in 1998.

Chapter XI

The Cycle Repeats

Those who do not learn from history
are doomed to repeat it.

Now at the beginning of the 21ˢᵗ Century, America seems determined to repeat the errors and sins of the past.

Re-segregation of the Public School System is the most damaging endeavor that America is undertaking. States throughout America are engaging in thinly veiled programs that have the affect of separating black and white American children.

Let us remember Proverbs 22:6 when we discuss educating children.

> *"Train up a child in the way he should go: and when his is old, he will not depart from it."*

> —(Proverbs 22:6)

A new segregation of the public school system is emerging throughout the southern United States where desegregation and busing was mandated by the United States Supreme Court in the 1954 Brown v. Board of Education of Topeka, Kansas decision.

Systematic attempts to undermine the 1954 desegregation decision have been implemented from the time it was made. The Republican administrations of United States Presidents Richard M. Nixon, Ronald Regan, and George Bush appointed conservative judges who over the years basically dismantled the court-ordered desegregation plans.

In 1971, over 16 years after the Supreme Court ordered public schools to desegregate, the Swann v. Board of Education Supreme Court case made court-ordered busing a national issue and functional mechanism to achieve school desegregation.

Twenty years later in the early 1990's, with more conservative judges in the courts, a series of United States Supreme Court decisions have made returning public schools to *Local Control,* the 21st Century euphemism for *States Rights,* a constitutional priority.

The end result of these new Supreme Court decisions is that once schools are returned to local control, it's like *putting the fox in the hen house* – the same separate or segregationist policies return that existed under Plessy v. Ferguson.

The new term used by white Christian Americans to help re-establish a segregated public school system is *"neighborhood schools".* The theory is that children are better served when they can attend schools near their homes.

White American parents stand boldly and self-righteously in public school meetings and declare that they don't want their children in classes with *"those children."* When a concerned black American parent challenged a white parent to state whom they were referring to as *"those children"*, it was clear that those children were little black American boys and girls.

Let us look at the real America.

Segregated churches encourage segregated neighborhoods and housing patterns. Segregated neighborhoods, under the *neighborhood school* concept, leads to segregated schools. Segregated schools will take America back to the segregated, divided America that existed from the time of The Reconstruction through the 1960s.

The facts and statistics document this re-segregation. The information provided in the Civil Rights Project conducted at Harvard University shows that the proportion of black American students in majority-white public schools has dropped dramatically over the last 14 years from 43.5 percent to 32.7 percent.

In the northern states, the prospect of integrated public schools is even worse. The most segregated schools in the nation are actually in the North: New York, California, Michigan and Illinois have the lowest percentages of black American students in majority-white schools.

True school integration was neutralized in the North by another United States Supreme Court decision: Milliken v. Bradley (1974). In this decision the Supreme Court blocked efforts of inter-district, city-suburban desegregation remedies as a means to integrate racially isolated city schools. The Supreme Court prohibited remedies to integrate predominantly black American inner cities with predominantly white American suburbs. In other words, "white flight"—

moving from integrating neighborhoods in the inner city to predominantly white suburbs—was an effective means to keep black children and white children separate and apart. White flight in essence facilitated and encouraged segregation.

In the North the plan was: *don't bus them (black students) out; we won't bus ours (white students) in.*

According to the Harvard Civil Rights Project:

> *"Anyone who thinks that the Supreme Court does not make a difference should look at the quarter century of decline in the segregation of Southern schools through the late 1980s, the continual, year-by-year growth in segregation since the Court authorized ending desegregation plans in 1991, as well as the impact of the court's 5-4 decision against city-suburban desegregation in 1974."*

The decisions of the United States Supreme Court in the last quarter of the 20th Century in undoing social, political, and educational advancement by black Americans is similar in spirit, intent, and fact to decisions of this same court in the last quarter of the 19th Century.

Election Fraud

The founding fathers in setting up the American democracy assumed that white Americans would always be in the majority. In this way, those who had the power and resources, namely white Christian citizens, would be able to legitimize their agenda by a majority vote of the electorate.

Anytime there was a threat that any group other

than the white Christians in power might be able to mobilize a voting majority, steps would be taken to neutralize that threat.

For example, in the United States Constitution as adopted by the founding fathers, black American slaves were defined as 3/5 's of a person to maintain a majority in the southern states where the number of slaves might equal or exceed the number of white American.

After the Civil War, and the Fifteenth Amendment to the Constitution giving black Americans the right to vote, white Americans in power systematically undermined the voting rights of black Americans.

Publicly sanctioned actions from threats and intimidation to death kept black Americans from exercising their constitutional right to vote from the end of the Civil War in 1865 through the 1960's. In fact, the 1965 Voting Rights acknowledged this voting reality of black American voters and attempted to remedy it.

Since the one-man, one-vote concept is the cornerstone of American democracy, white Americans in power develop new innovative ways to manipulate the voting process. This is especially true as black Americans, Hispanic Americans and other minorities in America are on track to collectively become the majority citizenry.

A prime example is the 2000 presidential election in which serious charges of voter fraud, manipulation, and undercounting of the votes in certain areas of Florida, a southern state, were virtually ignored by the white Americans in power as the United States Supreme Court awarded the presidency to George W. Bush.

Voting irregularities in Ohio, a northern state, were again ignored in the 2004 presidential elections.

Since democracy is a *winner-take-all* election and governmental process, the white Americans in power will do whatever it takes to win the elections necessary to legitimize their agenda—especially when their agenda is contrary to the popular good and benefit.

Electronic Voting

Electronic voting is the latest scheme endorsed by the white Americans in power to control the voting of all American citizens. The idea of replacing paper ballots with electronic machines, many of which do not give receipts to show if the machine properly registered the voter's wishes, is a backdoor means to steal elections.

If these *Electronic Voting* machines are put in place throughout America, there will come a time when the white Americans in power will be able to obtain a majority of votes for any issue or candidate while, no voter, candidate, or institution will be able to challenge the accuracy of the numbers. These *Electronic Voting* machines will enable the white Americans in power to maintain their power in spite of being a minority in population.

Think about it. If computer hackers can penetrate the computers in the United States Defense Department and other so-called secure organizations, hacking into and manipulating *Electronic Voting* machines is relatively easy. Even worse, through *Electronic Voting*, American citizens will be putting their government—their trust in their government—in the hands of the companies that develop, produce, and maintain such *Electronic Voting* machines.

Follow the party, persons, or organizations seeking to implement *Electronic Voting*, and you will find the culprits who will sooner or later use this instrument to steal elections and further their agendas.

Electronic Voting will be the new way to disenfranchise black Americans, poor Americans, and eventually all Americans.

America is repeating the same mistakes of the past. It is segregating the public school system, but yet expecting a different result in the future. It is disenfranchising its citizens, and yet expecting them to have faith and trust in the government.

But most of all, America has fallen prey to the principle of tyrants and despots:

He who has the gold rules.

Chapter XII

Where Do We Go From Here?

Moral Authority

The question arises: "Does America have the *Moral Authority* to promote life, liberty, and the pursuit of happiness to other people and countries when it still has not and cannot implement, promote and guarantee those same inalienable rights to its own citizens—black Americans?"

As America dominates the world stage, it becomes absolutely necessary, to resolve the spiritual and moral contradictions that undermine its international credibility. When we look at the past, the vile and brutal things this country—white Americans in power—has done historically to its black American citizens, we see that America does not enter the international arena with *Clean Hands*.

America itself is guilty of many of the very brutalities and sins of which it accuses other nations and people.

I am reminded of the words of Jesus:

> *"Judge not, that ye be not judged. For with*
> *what judgment ye judge, ye shall be judged:*
> *and with what measure ye mete, it shall be*
> *measured to you again."*

> *"And why beholdest thou the mote*
> *(speck) that is in thy brother's eye, but con-*
> *siderest not the beam that is in thine own*
> *eye?"*
> *"Or how wilt thou say to thy brother,*
> *Let me pull out the mote out of thine eye; and,*
> *behold, a beam in thine own eye?"*
> *"Thou hypocrite, first cast out the*
> *beam out of thine own eye; and then shalt*
> *thou see clearly to cast out the mote out of thy*
> *brother's eye."*
>   —(Matthew 7:1-5)

Where is America?
Did it fade into yesterday?
Is America still captive to the *Paradigm of Slavery*?

America has become a starkly divided nation on many levels. There are divisions between white and black, rich and poor, the powerful and the powerless, and between Hispanic and non-Hispanic.

We must approach the future of America in a historical context. Born on July 4, 1776, this country has been on the world scene for a little over 225 years. This brief time period is but a blip on the historical scale by which countries, governments, and cultures are measured.

When compared with great political structures,

as the great society of ancient Egypt that could list a continuous chain of Pharaohs covering a period of nearly 3000 years in a temple at Abydos, or a Chinese culture that built the great wall stretching 3,000 miles 200 years before the birth of Christ, America's 230 year existence is too short a time to be worthy of the arrogance and its arrogant claims to be the greatest nation on earth.

If America does not have an epiphany, a total recapitulation, a confession of her sins, apology and atonement, then she will meet the same fate as other cultures and societies that were built on hubris, deception, lies, and injustice.

If America does not replace the *Paradigm of Slavery* with a *Paradigm of Freedom and Justice*, then, it is,

> *"...likened unto a foolish man, which built his house upon the sand: And the rain descended, and the floods came, and the winds blew, and beat upon that house; and it fell: and great was the fall of it"*
> —(Matthew 7:26, 27)

WHAT IS *AMERICA*?

The Power Estate

Is *America* the **America of the Power Estate**; predominantly rich white Christian Americans who control the government – who cater to large corporations where profit and greed are the only commandment? This America serves the god of **Profit, Power,** and **Pleasure.** Over the last 25 years, the income of the *Power Estate* has risen exponentially while the income of the average American has barely kept up with the standard of living. The current government of America, the *Power Estate*—the white Americans in power—is so dominated by big business and special interests that the plight and condition of most Americans, black or white, is of little interest—of black Americans— virtually non-existent.

The People Estate

Or, is *America* the ***America of the People Estate?***

An America so eloquently described in Dr. Martin Luther King's Dream:

An America that, *"...will rise up and live out the true meaning of its creed: "We hold these truths to be self-evident: that all men are created equal."*

An America where, *"..the sons of former slaves and the sons of former slave owners will be able to sit down together at the table of brotherhood."*

An America where, *"...little children will one day live in a nation where they will not be judged by the color of their skin but by the content of their character."*

An America where, *"we will be able to transform the jangling discords of our nation into a beautiful symphony of brotherhood."*

An America where, *"... all of God's children, black men and white men, Jews and Gentiles, Protestants and Catholics, will be able to join hands and sing in the words of the old Negro spiritual, "Free at last! free at last! thank God Almighty, we are free at last!"*

And so America

When the rains of truth
fall upon your naked body,
and the flood of tears
of a million captive souls
comes upon your barren shores,
and the winds of justice and equality
beat upon all that you have created,

Will America stand
before the eternal judge,
as a testament to the glory
of man's humanity to man?

Or, will it fall
as yet another broken promise
that men offer up to their God,
and be plowed into the earth
as though it never was?

**The answer America is not in our
stars,
but in ourselves**

Amen!

New Paradigm Publishing
P.O. Box 302
Wilmington, NC 28402
(800) 570-4009

I am interested in being a part of discussion groups on racism in America. Please visit: www.americatheracist.com for more information, or email to TalkBack@americatheracist.com

Please email us or visit the website to post instances of racism or positive instances of individuals rising above racism and truly making America one nation under God.

My name is_____

Address_____

City/State/Zip_____

Telephone #: (Home)_____(Bus)_____

I would like information about:

a.____   Workshops, Speeches and Lectures

b._____   Audio & Video tapes.

I would like to order_____copies of this book

@ $16.95/bk.— — — — — — — — —   _____

Sales Tax: NC residents (only) add 7%   _____

Shipping: Add $3.00 per book.   _____

Total Amount Enclosed (ck/mo)   _____

Make check payable to LifeSkill® Institute, Inc.

Make a copy of this page, fill it out, and send it to the above address.

www.ingramcontent.com/pod-product-compliance
Lightning Source LLC
Chambersburg PA
CBHW032043040426
42334CB00038B/543